Telling
the
Gospel

For Emmanuel Christian Church. And those three years with Luke.
Thanks for hanging in there!

BOB HARTMAN
Telling
the
Gospel

70 stories about Jesus to read out loud

MONARCH
BOOKS

Oxford, UK & Grand Rapids, Michigan, USA

First published in the UK in 2010 by Monarch Books
(a publishing imprint of Lion Hudson plc)
Wilkinson House, Jordan Hill Road, Oxford OX2 8DR, England
Tel: +44 (0)1865 302750 Fax: +44 (0)1865 302757
Email: monarch@lionhudson.com
www.lionhudson.com

ISBN 978 1 85424 961 6

Distributed by:
UK: Marston Book Services, PO Box 269,
Abingdon, Oxon, OX14 4YN
USA: Kregel Publications, PO Box 2607,
Grand Rapids, Michigan 49501

The text paper used in this book has been made from wood independently
certified as having come from sustainable forests.

British Library Cataloguing Data
A catalogue record for this book is available from the British Library.

Printed and bound in the UK by MPG Books.

Contents

The Whole Story

Introduction

Strictly speaking, I suppose that this reading doesn't actually belong in a book called *Telling the Gospel*. As you will see, it starts well before the beginning of the book of Luke. But without it, the book of Luke doesn't make nearly so much sense.

I'm convinced that it's not only people outside of the church, but those within, as well, who don't have a clear picture of the Big Story. And without that picture, the individual stories lack context and meaning. There is an overarching narrative in the Bible – a story arc into which each individual narrative fits. And this reading is an attempt to tell that Big Story as simply and concisely as possible. I have used it in churches and schools and training events, and each time I have seen the light-bulbs go on and heard many people say "Aha!" and the "So that's how it fits together!"

Without this story, all that follows is at risk of being turned into a collection of moral tales and fables. In fact, I would argue that what I call the Aesopization of the Bible is to blame for much of the misunderstanding that people, Christian and non-Christian alike, have about this amazing book. So let's start here, with the Big Story, and let that story set the context for the stories to come.

> TELLING TIPS: Most of the actions are done with the teller's hands. I have put them in parentheses after each line to help you along the way (I've almost done this piece enough times to remember what goes where, but I still find it helpful to have the cues). It's important that you teach the "chorus" to everyone first and run through it a couple of times with them. And make sure that you eyeball them the first couple of times you want them to come in, so they know how it works. And, yes, feel free to change or add to the actions.

Chorus:

Worship God *(hands raised in praise)*.
Respect yourself *(hands on chest)*.
Love one another *(hands clasped)*.
Make good use of the world *(make shape of world)*.

So God made the world,
And his voice was like a pair of hands *(put finger to mouth, then hold out hands)*.

Day One *(one finger)*: Light and Dark *(use hands to make two spaces)*.
Day Two *(two fingers)*: Sea *(wavy motion)*, Sky *(make big arc with hand above)*, and Space *(higher arc)*.
Day Three *(three fingers)*: Earth, hard as Rock *(fist)*, and from the earth, green growing things *(with other hand, grow plant from behind)*.
Day Four *(four fingers)*: Sun *(sunburst with one hand)*, Moon *(make crescent shape with two hands)*, and Stars *(pick out stars with fingers)*.
Day Five *(five fingers)*: Sea Animals *(fish motion)* and Sky Animals *(bird motion)*.
Day Six *(six fingers)*: Land Animals *(bunny)*. And finally, and best of all, Man and Woman *(a finger for each – one on each hand)*, Adam and Eve, made in God's image.

And God looked at it all and saw that it was GOOD *(thumbs up)*.
And he said:

Worship God,
Respect yourself,
Love one another,
Make good use of the world.

And on Day Seven, God rested *(head on hands)*.

But then the serpent, a sly and crafty creature *(wiggly finger on one hand)*, spoke to Eve *(upright finger on other hand)*.
"So God told you not to eat that fruit? Well, I say, take a bite – and you will be just like him."

So Eve took a bite *(upright finger on one hand bites hand shaped like apple – fist with thumb sticking out the top)*.
And Adam did, too *(do the same – reversing hands)*.

And suddenly everything was mixed up *(mixed-up hands)*.
They were ashamed of themselves *(finger on each hand – look at each other and run from each other)*.
They used each other *(fingers fight)*.
They worshipped the world *(fingers bow – "man" finger bows down three times and says, "Power, Wealth, Fame". Then "woman" finger bows down once and says "Shoes!")*
And when God came calling, they did not worship him, they ran from him and hid *(fingers run and hide)*.

So God came up with a plan – a plan for his hands – to make things like they were, and maybe even better, so that once again all would be good *(thumbs up)*.

Worship God,
Respect yourself,
Love one another,
Make good use of the world.

He chose a man *(single finger)*, a man named Abraham, and took him from his home to another land *(grab finger with other hand and move it)*. "I will bless the world through your family," God promised.
And he gave him a son called Isaac *(another finger joins first one)*.
He gave Isaac two sons, Jacob and Esau *(two more fingers join)*.
He gave Jacob twelve sons *(hands and toes gag: count Abraham's kin up to that point on your fingers – one man, then his one son, then his two sons, then you come to twelve sons – so you start counting on fingers, run out, then lift a foot in the air as if you are adding with toes)*.
And when a famine came, he took one son and then the whole family to Egypt *(make a "Walk Like an Egyptian" shape)*, so they would be safe.
And there the family grew – grew so large that Pharaoh became frightened and turned them into slaves *(hands holding bars)*.
So God used his strong hand *(raised fist)* to set them free.
He made a way through the Red Sea *(parting motion with hands)*.

He watered them *(hands water garden – watering pot)*.
And fed them *(hands like feeding a child)*.
And led them through the desert with Fire *(flame motion)* and Cloud
    (make puffy cloud shape with hands).
And he gave them rules to live by. Rules that said:

Worship God,
Respect yourself,
Love one another,
Make good use of the world.

And finally he brought them back to the land he gave to Abraham *(move
    finger with other hand again)*, where everything should have been good
    (thumbs up)!
But because they were also children of Adam and Eve, things got all
    mixed up again *(repeat mixed-up motion)*:
And they did things to shame themselves *(as before)*.
And they used each other *(as before)*.
And they worshipped the world *("woman" finger bows three times and
    says, "Power, Wealth, Fame", and "man" finger bows once and says,
    "Ferrari!")*
And they ran from God and hid *(as before)*.

So God called upon his "right-hand men" *(hold right hand high)*:
Judges *(bring down gavel motion)* like Gideon and Samson,
Good Kings *(crown of two hands on head)* like David and Hezekiah,
Prophets *(hand from lips – outward)* like Elijah, Isaiah and Jeremiah,
To lead them back to him.
But the more he reached out to his people *(one hand reaches)*, the more
    they ran away *(the other moves away)*.
And finally he had to let them go off to slavery again *(hands on bars
    again)* – off to Babylon – for seventy long years.

He brought them back, at last *(one hand brings back the other)*.

And then God went quiet *("Shhh!" motion – finger to lips)*, very quiet, for 400 years. It takes time to make a plan – a good plan, that is – and this one was a doozie!

If his people wouldn't come to him, then he would go to them.
So he put on hands *(pretend to put on hands – like gloves)*. The hands of a man called Jesus.

And he spoke through those hands and reached out through those hands.
And those hands were just like a voice *(finger from lips outward again)*.

"Worship God," he said. And his hands cleansed the temple of injustice and greed *(pushing-away motion)*.
"Respect yourself," he said. And his hands welcomed the outcast *(pulling-in, welcoming motion)*.
"Love one another," he said. And his hands healed the sick *(gentle touch)* and forgave the sinner *(holding motion)* and brought enemies together *(clasp hands)*.
"Make good use of the world," he said. And his hands stilled the storm *(violent hands, then still)* and turned water into wine *(pouring motion, then glass raised)*.

His people should have been happy. Everything should have been good *(thumbs up)*.
But because they were children of Adam and Eve, everything got mixed up again *(mixed-up motion)*.

And they took those hands.
And bound those hands *(hands crossed)*.
And drove nails through those hands *(finger in each palm – or hammering motion)*.
And pinned them to a cross *(hands held out in crucifixion position)*.
And when those hands were quiet and still, they folded those hands *(fold hands)* and put them in a tomb *(roll stone in front)*.

One day passed, then two, then three *(count with fingers – 1, 2, 3)*.

And because they were God's hands, no tomb could hold them. No
power could still them forever.
So they rolled the stone away (roll stone away), and burst out of the
tomb *(bursting motion with hands)*.

And when he went to see his friends, Jesus said, "Don't be afraid, it's me.
Look, see the nail-prints" *(show nail-prints – 1, 2)*. "These are my
hands" *(hold out hands)*.
And before he left them, before he waved goodbye *(wave)*, he put his
message in their hands *(finger to lips to hands)*. "Go," he said, "go tell
everyone:

Worship God,
Respect yourself,
Love one another,
Make good use of the world."

And so they did,
From Judea
To Samaria,
To the ends of the earth *(point to a spot, then one further away, then one
further still)*,
To you and me *(point to audience and then to self)*.

And now we are his hands *(hold out hands)*
To do his work.
And one day, when he returns, he will wipe away all that is mixed up
(mixed-up motion), and every tear with it *(wipe tear from cheek)*.
And the work of his hands *(hand held high)* and the work of our hands
(hand held low) will make a new heaven *(two hands held high coming
down)* and a new earth *(make shape of world)*.

And we will worship him,
And respect ourselves,
And love one another,
And make good use of that new world forever.

Give yourself a hand! *(applaud)*

14

Questions

1. Are there any events you would mention that go unmentioned in this account? Why?

2. Are there any events you would describe differently? How?

3. Who do you think might benefit from hearing this account?

Angel Surprise

(Luke 1:26–38)

Introduction

This story was originally in my book *Angels, Angels All Around*. That book is out of print now, so I wanted to make sure that my favourite stories in that collection continued to be available (and not just on eBay!). This one might actually be my absolute favourite of that bunch. I know a lot of people like the Easter Angel story, but the thing I like about this one is the angel Gabriel. I realize that there is no way of knowing how an angel thinks or what an angel feels. Entering into that experience imaginatively was what lay at the heart of that book in the first place. But I found the idea that an angel might get tired of the shocked and petrified reaction to his sudden appearance really compelling. And also the idea that an angel might be capable of being shocked, in his own right.

It's a great piece for an early Advent service. Enjoy!

> **TELLING TIPS: This is definitely one to tell or read on your own. It could be read with actors miming the parts, but it would have to be done very sensitively.**

The angel Gabriel sat in the corner and watched.

The girl was only thirteen. Fourteen at most. Barely a woman, by the shape of her. With long, dark hair and bright olive skin. Not beautiful, but far from plain. Pretty.

Gabriel hugged his knees and scrunched himself back into the corner. The last thing he wanted to do was scare her, but that's what always seemed to happen when angels appeared. And maybe that's why Gabriel hated these surprise visits.

The girl was whistling now. Doing her ordinary, everyday tasks – as if this was some ordinary afternoon, and not the most extraordinary day of her life.

The angel rested his chin on his knees. Think, Gabriel, think. She's young. She's innocent. She's fragile. So how do you do it? How do you tell her that God is about to change her whole life, without scaring her to death?

Mary swept as she whistled. And as the dust motes danced in front of her broom, catching the sun and changing shape, Gabriel had an idea. What about a vision, he wondered. The dust rises and takes on the form of a man. "Mary," the dust-cloud-man says, "you are going to be the mother of the Son of God!"

Gabriel shook his head, then buried it in his arms. No, no, no, he decided. Still too scary. And besides, all it takes is a strong breeze, and the poor girl has to sweep her floors all over again!

It was too late now, anyway. Mary had put her broom away and was across the room, preparing dinner. Gabriel climbed up out of the corner and stretched. Then he followed her to the table.

Bread. She was making bread. And as Mary mixed the ingredients, another idea started to knead itself together and rise in Gabriel's head.

He could write the message in the flour on the table. Of course! A hand from heaven, like the one that scratched those letters on the wall in Babylon. But it would have to be brief, because there wasn't much time. Mary's parents were gone, and there was no telling when they'd come back through the door. He wouldn't want to be surprised in the middle of his message. Gabriel hated surprises!

But wait, thought Gabriel. Maybe he could be the one at the door. An unexpected visitor with an important message. But what if she got scared and slammed the door in his face? Or what if some passer-by saw them? (She'd have enough explaining to do when the baby arrived. She wouldn't want to have to make excuses for some mysterious stranger.)

Gabriel had run out of ideas. He was running out of time. So he sighed. A long frustrated angel sigh.

Perhaps it was that sigh. Maybe it was something else that Mary heard. For whatever reason, she spun around and seemed to hang suspended in the air for a second, her hair flung out behind her, her feet barely touching the floor. And her eyes, her eyes looked right into Gabriel's.

They should have looked right through him, but they didn't. Somehow she could see him. Somehow she knew he was there.

"Hello, Mary," he said finally, because there was nothing else to say. "God is with you, and wants to do something very special for you."

Mary didn't say anything. But she didn't faint, either. And that was a great relief to the angel. She just stood there, shaking ever so slightly, and stared at her guest.

"There's no need to be afraid," Gabriel assured her, although it was hard to know exactly what she was feeling. Was she trembling with fear? Or was it more like excitement? Gabriel couldn't tell. And he didn't like that one bit. This girl was nothing like what he had expected. This girl was a bit of a surprise.

"Look," he continued, "God is very pleased with you. So pleased, in fact, that he wants you to be the mother of a very special child – Jesus, the Messiah, the deliverer whom your people have been waiting for all these years."

Surely this would shock her, Gabriel thought. And he was ready to catch her if she should fall. But all she did was sit herself down to think. She played with the hem of her dress, folding and unfolding it. She twisted her hair.

Say something, thought Gabriel. Say anything!

And finally she did.

"I don't understand. How can this happen? How can I become someone's mother when I'm not yet someone's wife?"

This was the last question the angel expected. This girl wasn't hysterical. She wasn't even alarmed. Her question was plain, straightforward and practical.

So Gabriel answered her the best he could. "The Holy Spirit will visit you. You will be wrapped in the power of the Almighty. And you will give birth to the Son of God."

Mary had never heard of such a thing. And it showed. In her bright brown eyes it showed.

"God can do anything," said Gabriel. "Think about your cousin Elizabeth. Well past child-bearing age. Barren, by all accounts. And yet, she's expecting a son!"

Mary looked up at the angel and shook her head. She was still trying to take it in. But she wasn't afraid, he could tell that much. She was strong, this girl. A doer. A coper. A fighter. And when she finally weighed it all up, Gabriel knew what her answer would be even before she gave it. Those eyes of hers were shining, fierce and bold.

"I'll do it," she said. "I'll do it. I'll be whatever God wants me to be."

Gabriel nodded. Then he turned to leave. He reached out to open the curtain – the curtain between heaven and earth – and saw that his hand was trembling.

He turned back to look at Mary one last time. And in the mirror of her eyes, Gabriel saw one shocked angel face.

Mary smiled at him. He smiled back. Perhaps surprises aren't so bad after all, he thought.

Then Gabriel pulled the curtain behind him and said goodbye to the girl.

The girl who had surprised an angel.

And who would one day surprise the world.

Questions

1. Do you think that an angel can be shocked or surprised? Why or why not?

2. Why do you suppose that the popular picture of angels often paints them as bringers of comfort and calm and peace, when the biblical accounts almost always paint a picture of dread and fear?

3. What do you think of the portrayal of Mary in the story? Is there anything you disagree with? Anything you might have added to or subtracted from this account?

Mary Meets an Angel

(Luke 1:26–38)

Introduction

This is the first of many three-line-rhyming stories that you will find in this collection. So I might as well explain what I'm up to and how these work, right from the start.

I chanced upon this story form when I was asked to prepare a story for an all-age service several years ago. The organizers asked me to fill a nine-minute slot, and when I had written the story (a retelling of Paul and Barnabas's experience in the city of Lystra), I found that it only lasted three minutes. Yes, that's right, I tripled it up so it would fit! But what I discovered was that the tripling of each line had some real benefits (apart from meeting my contractual obligation). In the first line of each couplet, three readings gives you the chance to milk that line of its meaning – to rephrase it each time in such a way that you can move the emphasis about. In the case of the second line in each couplet, repeating three times gives everyone the chance to "catch on" to how the participation works, to enjoy it that bit more, to really "get it". Best of all, it's simply a lot easier to memorize, and is a nice way to get a lot of stories under your belt without a lot of work!

TELLING TIPS: I have put the participation ideas in the text, to make it easier to find them as you lead your group. They are only there once, following the first line in the second group of three – but you are meant to do the actions each time you repeat that action line.

It's really helpful to teach all the actions before you start the story, even though you will be repeating them several times later. It helps set the mood, particularly if you have fun with your group as you teach them. I will often teach the actions and then ask the group to guess which story it is, based upon those actions! Oh, and it's really important to practise these before you do them – particularly so you get the rhythm right and fit the words into each line.

1. An angel appeared to a girl named Mary,
   An angel appeared to a girl named Mary,
   An angel appeared to a girl named Mary,
   Bright white like a lightning beam.
   (Draw shape of lightning bolt with finger; could also make thundery sound with it.)
   Bright white like a lightning beam.
   Bright white like a lightning beam.

2. "Don't be afraid," the angel said to Mary.
   "Don't be afraid," the angel said to Mary.
   "Don't be afraid," the angel said to Mary.
   "I have good news for you. Please don't scream."
   (Scream! Aaaaah!)
   "I have good news for you. Please don't scream."
   "I have good news for you. Please don't scream."

3. "You're going to have a baby!" the angel explained.
   "You're going to have a baby!" the angel explained.
   "You're going to have a baby!" the angel explained.
   "You'll need a robe with expandable seams!"
   (Two hands gripping and pulling apart.)
   "You'll need a robe with expandable seams!"
   "You'll need a robe with expandable seams!"

4. "But how can that be?" said Mary to the angel.
   "But how can that be?" said Mary to the angel.
   "But how can that be?" said Mary to the angel.
   "I haven't married the man of my dreams."
   (Two hands to face, look upward dreamily – or point to pretend wedding ring.)
   "I haven't married the man of my dreams."
   "I haven't married the man of my dreams."

5. "God will be the father," the angel said to Mary.
   "God will be the father," the angel said to Mary.
   "God will be the father," the angel said to Mary.
   "As impossible as that might seem."
   (A big "Wow!")
   "As impossible as that might seem."
   "As impossible as that might seem."

6. "You will call the baby Jesus," the angel said to Mary.
   "You will call the baby Jesus," the angel said to Mary.
   "You will call the baby Jesus," the angel said to Mary.
   "Come to save the world and make it new and clean."
   (Scrubbing motion.)
   "Come to save the world and make it new and clean."
   "Come to save the world and make it new and clean."

7. "Then I'll do it," said Mary. "I'll be God's loyal servant."
   "Then I'll do it," said Mary. "I'll be God's loyal servant."
   "Then I'll do it," said Mary. "I'll be God's loyal servant."
   And the sparkle in her eye showed she was keen.
   (Point to eye, make "ding" sound.)
   And the sparkle in her eye showed she was keen.
   And the sparkle in her eye showed she was keen.

8. Then the angel went away, leaving Mary there to wonder,
   Then the angel went away, leaving Mary there to wonder,
   Then the angel went away, leaving Mary there to wonder,
   Wonder what this new adventure would mean.
   (Finger to chin – "Hmmm?")
   Wonder what this new adventure would mean.
   Wonder what this new adventure would mean.

Questions

1. There are some Christians, of course, who don't believe this particular story or who see it as a kind of myth. What do you think about that and why do you think this story is important?

2. Put yourself in Mary's place. How might you have responded to the angel's appearance and his request?

3. This story only appears in Luke's Gospel. Why do you think that is?

Two Women, One Door

(Luke 1:39–45)

Introduction

Telling the Christmas story is a task that most ministers face each year. The same is probably true for teachers (that annual assembly!) and any church leaders who work with children. The trick is to find new and creative ways to tell a story that most of your audience have heard before. Every time I think I've run out of ways to do that, something else comes along. This is an example. Sure, it's only part of the story, but it's a part that often gets overlooked. This meeting, that Luke alone tells us about, must have been really interesting. So I thought it was worth exploring. Perhaps it will help you to find a new way of looking at this narrative as well.

TELLING TIPS: One for doing on your own, or perhaps with a partner – one to deal with what happens on Mary's side of the door, and one to deal with what happens on Elizabeth's.

There were two women. Two cousins. With two secrets. And one wooden door between them.

The woman on the outside of the door was barely a woman at all. She looked much more like a girl. And as she raised her hand to knock, she wondered, "How shall I tell her? How shall I tell my cousin about this thing that has happened to me?"

And, in an instant, it all came back to her.

The angel's greeting. Her startled shock. And the angel's message that made her shock more startling still:

"You will have a baby. God's own special Son. And you will call him Jesus, for he is coming to save the world."

"How?" she'd asked. "How can this be, when I am not even married?"

And the angel's answer – that God's own Spirit would somehow come upon her – was no less troubling.

Would her cousin be shocked, as well? Perhaps not. And that was why she had come. For the angel had said that her cousin was expecting a baby, too – even though she was well past child-bearing age. So maybe she, of all people, might somehow understand what had happened.

Otherwise, there was no way to make sense of this. No way to explain it. God wanted to do something wonderful, and amazing, and impossible for her. That was all the girl could say.

And with that, Mary knocked on the door.

The woman on the other side raised her head at the sound and moved slowly across the room. She was an older woman. Much, much older. Too old to have a baby, for sure. But her swollen belly said different.

And as she made her way to the door, she wondered how she would explain that belly to her cousin. Her quick rehearsal sounded ridiculous:

"An angel appeared to my husband, while he was working in the temple. The angel told him that we would have a baby boy. He told him to call the baby John, and that John would be the one to prepare our people for the coming of the Messiah – God's own special one. And, furthermore, because my husband found this story just a bit far-fetched, the angel struck him dumb, and he's been sitting here, for the past six months, quiet as a stone."

The woman shook her head. "She'll think I'm mad! She'll turn around and run out of here like it was a crazy house."

Then she looked at her silent husband and he smiled. She smiled back. And with that, Elizabeth opened the door.

And as soon as she did – the moment she laid her eyes on Mary – her baby kicked. Not a gentle kick. But a big, hard kick. A kick like he was trying to kick his way out. A kick like he was dancing in there. Like he was dancing for joy!

And that's when Elizabeth knew – without Mary having to say a word.

"You're going to have a baby, cousin, aren't you? And he's the one, isn't he? God's own special Son! And here you are, at my door, to honour me with your presence! Come in, and trust that all God has promised you will come true."

So Mary went in. And the two women shared their stories. Two women.

Two cousins. No longer two secrets like a door between them. Just the promise of two special sons.

Questions

1. Find three or four words to describe Mary in this situation.

2. Find three or four words to describe Elizabeth.

3. Go on, then – find three or four words to describe Zechariah. And why do you think Luke includes this story?

"Magnificent" – Mary's Song

(Luke 1:46–55)

Introduction

In *Telling the Bible*, I included several "Songs in Search of a Tune". And I suppose this is one of those. There aren't that many in this book, so I didn't think it was worth creating a separate category, but I like this one, so I thought I'd put it in.

I have tried to be faithful to the spirit and the sense of what we have come to call the *Magnificat*. That's one of the reasons the song/poem is in the third person (it works addressed to God, as well, and I have put that version at the end), because that's how Mary phrases it.

I don't see any problem with just reading it as a version of the passage, but feel free to add a tune, if you like!

> **TELLING TIPS: Nothing much, really. You might want to have your group read the chorus as one while you do the verses.**

Mighty One, Holy One, merciful forever.
Age to age, each generation spent.
Faithful One, Patient One, whose love cannot be severed.
There's no other word for him: Magnificent.

My soul cries out, my spirit sings
In praise of God, my Saviour,
Who looks at me and sees me as I am,
Then lifts me up on angel wings,
Hands that never waver,
And makes me part of his eternal plan.

Mighty One, Holy One, merciful forever.
Age to age, each generation spent.
Faithful One, Patient One, whose love cannot be severed.
There's no other word for him: Magnificent.

He shakes the proud and breaks the crown
And makes the strong man stumble.
He sends the rich man begging in the street,
Then reaches down and from the ground
Lifts up the poor and humble
And welcomes them to his forever feast.

Mighty One, Holy One, merciful forever.
Age to age, each generation spent.
Faithful One, Patient One, whose love cannot be severed.
There's no other word for him: Magnificent.

(Second-person version:)
Mighty One, Holy One, merciful forever.
Age to age, each generation spent.
Faithful One, Patient One, whose love cannot be severed.
There's no other word for you: Magnificent.

My soul cries out, my spirit sings
In praise of God, my Saviour.
You look at me and see me as I am
Then lift me up on angel wings,
Hands that never waver,
And make me part of your eternal plan.

Mighty One, Holy One, merciful forever.
Age to age, each generation spent.
Faithful One, Patient One, whose love cannot be severed.
There's no other word for you: Magnificent.

You shake the proud and break the crown
And make the strong man stumble.
You send the rich man begging in the street

Then reach right down and from the ground
Lift up the poor and humble
And welcome them to your forever feast.

Mighty One, Holy One, merciful forever.
Age to age, each generation spent.
Faithful One, Patient One, whose love cannot be severed.
There's no other word for you: Magnificent.

Questions

1. What would you say is the main point of this passage? (Feel free to use either this retelling or the passage itself to come up with your answer.)

2. What events in the history of Israel are reflected in this passage?

3. What does the passage mean for us? For you?

"And Here He Comes" – Zechariah's Song

(Luke 1:67–80)

Introduction

All right, then – here's the other "Song in Search of a Tune". It just made sense, as I looked at this one and the one before, to cast them in some kind of song style. So the same thing goes for this one as the last one. Oh, and the "horn" thing refers to a ram's horn (that powerful butting instrument with which he assaults his foes) and not to a tuba (another kind of instrument altogether).

> **TELLING TIPS: Again, if you're going to read it, have your group do the chorus and you do the verses.**

And here he comes, Strong Horn,
Here he comes, Mighty Lord,
Here he comes to face the evil in our land,
Here he comes, Strong Horn,
Here he comes, Mighty Lord,
Here he comes to save the people from its hand.

He comes to show us mercy,
He comes to set us free,
He comes because he does just what he says,
He comes to make us holy,
He comes to make us good,
He comes to help us serve him all our days.

And here he comes, Strong Horn,
Here he comes, Mighty Lord,
Here he comes to face the evil in our land,
Here he comes, Strong Horn,
Here he comes, Mighty Lord,
Here he comes to save the people from its hand.

He comes to bring salvation,
He comes, forgiving sin,
He comes, his mercy rising in the east,
He comes to light the darkness,
He comes to conquer death,
He comes to help us walk in paths of peace.

And here he comes, Strong Horn,
Here he comes, Mighty Lord,
Here he comes to face the evil in our land,
Here he comes, Strong Horn,
Here he comes, Mighty Lord,
Here he comes to save the people from its hand.

Questions

1. People today are sometimes put off by passages that emphasize God's power and might in violent terms. Why do you think that is so? And how do you feel about those passages?

2. Which Old Testament references do you find in this passage?

3. What image would you use (in place of "horn") to describe God's power? What might be a better contemporary image?

This Story is Brought to You by the Letter G

(Luke 2:8–20)

Introduction

To tell a familiar story differently, and simply, yet tell it well – that's the trick. And you won't find a way to do that unless you experiment a bit. So here's one of these experiments. Use it if it works for you.

> **TELLING TIPS:** Teach your group actions for each of the G words and lead them in those actions at the start of each section. If you like, you can bring some of them back in when they are repeated in the final verse.
>
> - **Grazing – munching sound**
> - **Gazing – look up in the sky, dreamily**
> - **Gobsmacked – make a funny shocked expression**
> - **Good News – shout "Yeah!"**
> - **Glory – raise hands and shout "Glory!"**
> - **Go – move head quickly from one side to the other as if you are watching someone go!**
> - **Gossip – pretend whisper to your neighbour**

Grazing.
It starts off as a story about grazing.
Sheep on a hillside, grass grinding between their teeth.
And shepherds watching them graze.

Gazing.
That's where the story goes.
One of the shepherds looks up.
The sky splits. A slit in the starry curtain. And an angel bursts through.

Gobsmacked.
That's the best way to put it.
The shepherds shiver and shake. And the sheep (what do they know?)
just keep chewing.

"Good News!"
That's what the angel shouts.
And then "Don't be afraid.
Your Messiah, your Deliverer, your Saviour has come.
And you can find him in a town down the road."

And then *"Glory!"*
That's what the angel sings.
And a glorious chorus joins him.
"Glory to God on high.
Peace to men on earth."

Then they *Go.*
First the angels (who knows where?)
And then the shepherds.
Off to Bethlehem, to see their newborn king.

What next? *Gossip!*
They spread the news, then head back to the hills,
Where the sheep set to grazing again.
And they can't help but gazing again.
And giving God the Glory for his Good News.

Questions

1. What was your favourite "Nativity Play" experience (assuming you have one), and why?

2. What part of the Christmas story do you most enjoy?

3. What part of the Christmas story makes you go "Huh?"

Old Shepherd

(Luke 2:8–20)

Introduction

There are a lot of potential "what ifs" in the Bible, and this is one of them. It's unlikely, obviously, that something like this actually happened, but it does give the opportunity to let one familiar Bible story inform another and help us, perhaps, to better understand them both.

> **TELLING TIPS: Definitely one to do on your own. I dropped this into the end of a Christmas Candlelight Service originally, and it was really effective.**

The old shepherd climbed the hill like he'd climbed up hills a hundred times before. And as he climbed he looked, this way and that, for his one lost little lamb.

At the top of the hill he stopped to catch his breath. And that's when he saw the woman.

"I know you," he said, struggling for breath and surprised that the words had even come out. But he was so shocked to see her that he could not help himself.

"It has been many years," he went on. "But you are the woman, I'm sure of it. The woman the angel led us to. The woman in the stable."

The woman wiped the tears from her eyes and nodded. But she did not look at the old shepherd, not even for a second. For her gaze was fixed on her own little lamb. Fixed on him as he hung there in the air.

"And your baby?" the shepherd continued, following her gaze. "Is that your baby there?"

Again the woman nodded. Yes.

"The angel seemed so certain," mused the old man after a while. "The

Saviour. Christ. The Lord. That's what he told us. And that is why my companions and I ran with such haste to see you – with my own little boy leading the way. But, surely, the angel…"

"The angel was not wrong," the woman interrupted. "God was at work then, all those years ago. And God is at work now. I believe it. I must."

"But how?" whispered the shepherd. "How, in the face of this?"

"Hush," said the woman. "He's trying to speak."

"Today," said the man in the air. "Today," he said to the man hanging next to him. "Today, you will be with me in Paradise."

And as he watched, and as he listened, the old man's eyes filled with tears, as well.

"Do you see?" said the woman. "Even now. Even here. The angel's words ring true. Who else could make such a promise to a dying man? Who else would even care?"

"I must go," said the shepherd. "I have found what I was looking for."

"But you haven't told me," said the woman. "Whatever happened to your son? The little boy with the lamb?"

"Yes, well…" the old man faltered. "I suppose you could say that he fell in with the wrong crowd and wandered away."

"I see," said the woman. "I'm sorry. Do you know where he is now?"

"Now?" answered the shepherd, looking one last time into the sky. "Now he is on his way to Paradise. I guess our angel was right, after all."

And with that he turned and climbed back down the hill, like he'd climbed down hills a hundred times before.

Questions

1. Talk about a time when you wondered if God's promise would ever come true.

2. How are Mary and the old shepherd different? How are they much the same?

3. What do the promises the angels sang about mean to you?

The Most Important Thing?

(Luke 2)

Introduction

Just a question. Just an observation. Just a little Christmas story.

> **TELLING TIPS: You could either read this on your own, or you could intersperse the different vignettes with songs and prayers and use this as the basis of a carol or Christmas Eve service.**

The senator slammed his hand against the wall.

"Fools! Idiots!" he shouted, as a servant stuck his head in the door and then quickly retreated.

"My proposal would have created a thousand jobs and given us a network of northern roads to be proud of. How could they have voted it down?"

The door squeaked open again. It was the senator's wife, this time.

"Darling," she asked quietly. "Is something wrong?"

"Everything is wrong!" he bellowed back. "I'm trying to initiate a desperately important project, and all the Senate can think about is Caesar's latest diversion. Let's see how big we are. Let's see how powerful we are. Let's have a *census*! So we count up the tribes in Scotland, the barbarians in Gaul, the peasants in Palestine, and miss the chance of a lifetime!"

He slammed his hand against the wall again.

"It simply amazes me how intelligent people can focus on some irrelevancy and lose sight of the most important thing."

The soldiers stood to attention before their commander.

"Well done, men!" he shouted. "We fought hard. We sustained losses.

But in the end we prevailed. And, thanks to you, the empire will be safer for it. I know it's getting late and most of you are ready for a well-deserved rest, but I simply wanted to take this opportunity to congratulate you on a job well done."

Suddenly, behind the commander and far above his crested helmet, something shot across the sky. Most of the soldiers ignored it. But one, right at the front, let his head follow after its shining tail.

"Soldier!" barked the commander. "That's right, you there, in front. What are you staring at?"

The soldier jumped. "Nothing, Sir. Well, a star, Sir. I've never seen anything like it, Sir."

"I'll show you stars!" shouted the commander. "Sergeant, take this man away. A good hard beating should remind him that an order is an order, and that obedience, and not star-gazing, is the most important thing."

The merchant pounded his fist on the door.

"What do you mean there's no room in the stable? I've been riding all day. My horse is tired. And I have to leave first thing in the morning. I've got a business to run!"

"I'm sorry." said the innkeeper. "I had no idea you would be coming. There was this couple, you see…"

"No idea!" the merchant growled. "No idea? I've been staying here for how long now? Ten years? Popping in and out as the need arose. Always paying my bills."

And then he took a deep breath to compose himself. Bethlehem was full and the first order of business was to find a place for the night.

"Look, I'll forget about this little embarrassment, and I'll continue to bring you my business. Just toss that couple out and make room for my horse!"

The innkeeper thought for a moment. He really did. But then he shook his head.

"I can't. I just can't. She just had a baby, you see. I'm sorry."

"You'll be sorry, all right," grumbled the merchant. "Because this is the last time that I or any of my associates will be setting foot in this place. You have obviously forgotten the first rule of business. The customer comes first. That's the most important thing."

The most important thing. Sometimes it happens in the least important place, among the most unimportant people.

A son is born. Hardly anyone notices. But nearly 2,000 years later, when the empire is a memory, the battle a footnote, and the profits all spent, the son still lives at the heart of a culture, directs and inspires the lives of millions, and sits at the right hand of God himself.

The most important thing? It still has to do with that baby. And it still happens in the most obscure places and within the most obscure lives. Wherever we let him take control and use us to do his will. Whenever we take our eyes off those other "important things", follow the starry trail and make room for that child in the stable of our hearts.

Questions

1. So what "most important things" get in the way of you seeing the child in the manger at Christmas-time?

2. Do these competing priorities have any place?

3. What do you do each year to ensure that Christmas is celebrated as a Christian holiday in your home?

A Night the Stars Danced for Joy

(Luke 2:8–20)

Introduction

Here's another story from *Angels, Angels All Around* that I wanted to keep...
well... around.

TELLING TIP: One to do on your own.

The shepherd, the shepherd's wife and the shepherd boy lay on their
backs on top of the hill. Their hands were folded behind their heads, and
their feet stretched out in three directions like points on a compass. Their
day's work was done. Their sheep had dropped off to sleep. And they had
run out of things to say.

So they just lay there on top of that hill and stared lazily into the night
sky.

It was a clear night. There were no clouds for shy stars to hide behind.
And the bolder stars? For some reason, they seemed to be shining more
proudly than any of the shepherds could remember.

Suddenly, what must have been the boldest star of all came rushing
across the sky, dancing from one horizon to the other and showing off its
sparkling serpent's tail.

"Shooting star," said the boy dreamily. "Make a wish."

The shepherd and his wife said nothing. They were too old for games
and too tired tonight, even to say so.

But they were not too old for wishing.

The shepherd fixed his eyes on a cluster of stars that looked like a great
bear. And he thought about the cluster of scars on his leg – jagged
reminders of a battle he'd fought with a real bear long ago. A battle to
save his sheep.

There were other scars, too, mapped out like a hundred roads across his back. Souvenirs of his battles with that Great Bear, Rome. The land of Israel belonged to his people, not to the Roman invaders. So why should he bow politely to their soldiers and surrender his sheep for their banquets? Greedy tyrants. Uniformed thieves. That's what they were. And even their claw-sharp whips would not change his mind.

And so the shepherd made a silent wish. He wished for someone to save him. From violence. From greed. From bears.

The shepherd's wife had her eyes shut. This was the hardest time of the day for her. The time when there was nothing to do but try to fall asleep. The time when the wind carried voices back to her. Her voice and her mother's. Angry, bitter voices. Voices hurling words that hurt. Words she wished she'd never spoken. Words she couldn't take back now, because her mother was dead, and there was no chance to say she was sorry.

And so the shepherd's wife made a silent wish, too. She wished for peace, for an end to those bitter voices on the wind.

The shepherd boy grew tired of waiting.

"All right," he said finally. "I'll make a wish, then. I wish I wish I wish something interesting would happen for a change. Something exciting. I'm tired of just sitting on this hill night after night. I want something to laugh about. To sing and dance about."

The shepherd turned to look at his wife.

The shepherd's wife opened her eyes and shook her head.

But before either of them could say anything, something happened. Something that suggested the shepherd boy just might get his wish.

Like tiny white buds blossoming into gold flowers, the stars began to swell and spread, until their edges bled together and the sky was filled with a glowing blanket of light. And then that blanket of light began to shrink and gather itself into a brilliant, blinding ball that hung above them.

The shepherds dared not move. All they could do was stare into that light. They watched it slowly change again. Shining rays stretched into arms. Legs kicked out like white beams. And a glowing face blinked bright and burning. The light sprouted wings. It took the shape of an angel. And it spoke.

"Don't be afraid," the angel said, "but sing and dance for joy! I have good news for you. Today, in Bethlehem, your Saviour was born – the special one whom God promised to send you. Here's the proof: if you go to Bethlehem, you will find the baby wrapped in cloths and lying in a feed trough."

The shepherds were still too shocked to speak. But that didn't keep them from thinking.

"Don't be afraid?" thought the shepherd. "He's got to be joking."

"A baby in a feed trough?" thought the shepherd's wife. "Why, even our boy got better treatment than that."

"Sing and dance for joy?" thought the shepherd boy. "Now that's more like it!"

And as if in answer to the boy's thought, the angel threw his arms and legs wide, like the first step in some heavenly jig.

But instead, he flung himself – could it be? – into a thousand different pieces of light, pieces that scattered themselves across the dark blue of the night and landed where the stars had been. Pieces that turned into angels themselves, singing a song that the shepherds had never heard before, to a tune that had been humming in their heads forever.

"Glory to God in the highest!" the angels sang. "And peace on earth to all."

Some plucked at lyres. Some blew trumpets. Some beat drums. Some banged cymbals. There were dancers, as well – spinning and whirling, larking and leaping across the face of the midnight moon.

Finally, when the music could get no louder, when the singers could sing no stronger, when the dancers could leap no higher, when the shepherd's mouths and eyes could open no further, everything came to a stop.

As quickly as the angels had come, they were gone. The sky was silent and filled once more with twinkling stars. The shepherds lay there for a moment, blinking and rubbing their eyes.

At last the shepherd struggled to his feet. "Well," he said, "looks like we'd better find this baby."

The shepherd's wife pulled herself up, shook the grass off her robe and ran her fingers absently through her hair.

And the shepherd boy leaped eagerly to his feet and shouted, "Hooray!"

When they got to Bethlehem, things were just as the angel had said. A husband and a young mother. And a baby in a feed trough. A family much like the shepherd's, in fact. Was it possible, the shepherd wondered, for one so small, so poor, so ordinary, to be the Saviour? The Promised One?

Then the shepherd told the young mother about the angels. And that's when he knew. It was the look in her eyes. The look that said, "How wonderful!" but also, "I'm not surprised." There was something special going on here. The mother knew it. And now the shepherd and his family knew it, too.

"Well," said the boy as they made their way back to the hill, "my wish came true. Too bad you didn't make a wish."

The shepherd said nothing. But he ran one finger gently along his scars. Was he imagining things, or were they smaller now?

The shepherd's wife said nothing. She was listening. There were no bitter voices on the wind now. There were songs – heaven songs – and the cry of a newborn child.

"Glory to God in the highest!" she shouted suddenly.

"And peace to everyone on earth!" the shepherd shouted back.

Then the shepherd boy shouted too – "Hooray!" – and danced like an angel for joy.

Questions

1. Pure speculation, really – all that thinking and wondering of the shepherds. But which shepherd wondered the kind of thing you might have wondered?

2. How would you imagine/describe the sudden appearance of the angels?

3. Does the fact that the angels appeared to shepherds have any significance? What, do you think?

Three Wise Gamers

(Matthew 2:1–12)

Introduction

A couple of Christmases ago, when the Wii system was just coming out, my son and his two cousins stayed up all night, outside of a local store, to be the first in line for a new shipment of the devices. Their experience (watching the car park by night) triggered this contemporary retelling.

> **TELLING TIPS: A two-hander. Someone to read the Scripture passage and someone else to read the rest – who will need to do "voices", I think, to differentiate the characters.**

And there were shepherds living out in the fields nearby, keeping watch over their flocks by night.

And a family of four gathered round the Eat'N'Park midnight buffet.

And a couple of cops on patrol.

And three young gamers huddled in their sleeping-bags outside of Currys, hoping for that final Wii delivery.

And an angel of the Lord appeared to them, and the glory of the Lord shone around them, and they were terrified.

Somewhere, in the back, a waitress dropped a loaded tray. Plates of tuna melts and superburgers fell crashing to the floor. But no one clapped. Frozen as fat-free sorbet, they just stood there, staring at the wonder before them – smiley-cookie grins on their faces.

Choking on their donuts, the cops dropped their coffees and called for back-up.

And while two of the gamers tried to figure out if this was a Nintendo publicity stunt and what the bit rate would have to be to create that kind of effect, the third learned the true meaning of Wii and decided to take his sleeping blanket to the cleaners in the morning.

But the angel said to them, "Do not be afraid..."

"All right, then," said the father, setting his gravy biscuit down.
  "Hey, you touched that!" said his son. "You can't put it back!"

"Afraid? Who's afraid?" said the cop.
  "I'm feeling a little weepy, sir," said his partner.

"Cool, dude. Surround sound!" said the gamers.

"I bring you good news of great joy that will be for all the people," the angel went on. "Today in the town of David a Saviour has been born to you; he is Christ the Lord. This will be a sign to you: you will find a baby wrapped in cloths and lying in a manger."

"Can we see the baby?" asked the little girl.
  "Of course, dear," said the mum.
  The father shook his head. "It's getting late."
  "Can I finish my pudding first?" asked the son.

"Town of David," the cop barked into his radio. "That's right – Delta, Alpha, whatever 'V' and 'I' are, Delta."

"I think there's a level like this in *Zelda*," said one of the gamers.
  "Messiah thing. Special baby. I think you're right," said the third.
  "What's that smell?" asked the second.

Suddenly a great company of the heavenly host appeared with the angel, praising God and saying, "Glory to God in the highest, and on earth peace to men on whom his favour rests."

When the angels had left them and gone into heaven, the shepherds said to one another, "Let's go to Bethlehem and see this thing that has happened, which the Lord has told us about."

The family of four paid the bill and climbed into their mini-van.

"Bethlehem," said the father, pulling out. "I think that's in the next county. Ah well, we'll find it."

"Why don't you just ask the nice angels for directions, dear?" said the mum.

"Are we there yet?" asked the kids.

"Bethlehem!" barked the cop. "That's right. Beta, Epsilon, umm – ah, forget it." And he switched on the sirens and roared off.

"We can't go now," said the first gamer. "If we leave the line we'll never get our Wii."

"Maybe we could go later," said the second, "and bring the little dude a birthday present. I've got my Pokémon Gold that I don't use much any more."

"And I could give him *Young Merlin*," said the second.

"Look," said the third, fishing through his knapsack, "my Mum put a bottle of frankincense in here."

"Have no idea what that is, dude," said the first, "but frankly, you could use some incense. Phew!"

So they hurried off and found Mary and Joseph, and the baby, who was lying in a manger.

The shepherds.
   The family of four.
   The cops.
   And the three wise gamers.

Questions

1. What do you think would actually happen if the manifestations witnessed by the shepherds and wise men were witnessed today? What guesses would people make regarding their origin?

2. In the absence of Pokémon Gold, *Young Merlin* (get it? Myrhh-lin!), or a bottle of frankincense that miraculously appeared in your rucksack, what would you bring the Christ Child?

3. Would you rush off to Bethlehem, or turn over and go back to sleep?

The Tyrant's Tale

(Matthew 2:1–18)

Introduction

What do you think of when someone says "Christmas"? Stars and angels, right? Giving and joy and peace and goodwill!

The story of the first Christmas is filled with those images. But, like most stories, that story has a villain, too. A selfish and cruel villain who does everything he can to rob the story of its wonder. A villain with a dark story all his own.

I thought it would be interesting to set those stories side by side – the story of Herod and the story of the child he tried to kill. Not only because the stories are so different, but also because the difference offers a vivid illustration of the contrast between good and evil – between God's gift of life and one man's deadly ambition.

> **TELLING TIPS: Another one to tell on your own. This one needs some real practising to be effective. If you wanted to emphasize the difference between the two stories, you could, I suppose, have a different reader for each.**

The night was crisp and clear. The stars shone bright like candles. A mother cradled a child in her arms. And when she closed her eyes and listened, she could almost hear the angels sing.

The old man in the palace, however, wasn't interested in angels. Ghosts were his companions. And they followed him, now, wherever he went.

It hadn't always been this way. When he was young, there was just too much to do: a kingdom to win. Power to establish. And enemies, more than he could count, to be dealt with and disposed of. And even when the bodies piled up – like stones stacked for his brand-new temple – the ghosts stayed respectfully still.

How could he have known that they were just waiting – waiting for him to grow old and sick, waiting for him to grow tired, waiting for long and lonely winter nights?

The ghost of his uncle.

The ghost of his aunt.

The ghost of his wife, Mariamne.

The ghosts of his ambitious sons.

Murdered, each and every one. Murdered at his command. Murdered because they tried to take his throne.

"I am the King of the Jews!" he growled. Growled at the darkness. Growled at the walls. Growled at the noisy company of ghosts.

"I am the King of the Jews!" he growled again, "Herod. Herod the Great!"

The walls did not answer. The darkness stayed silent and deep. But a knock at the door startled the king and sent him shaking.

"Who is it?" he whispered. "What is it?" he called. And his heart slowed to a steady beat when a servant stuck his head into the room.

"Visitors, your majesty," the servant answered.

"At this hour?" the king shouted. "Tell them to go away!"

"But they say it is urgent, your majesty. They have travelled, day and night, all the way from Babylon, following a star! A star which, they say, will lead them to our newborn king."

Herod's heart started racing again. First the ghosts, and now this. Would he never be able to rest? "Then send them in," he commanded.

The night was still and peaceful. The angels kept their silent watch. The carpenter kissed the baby and told his wife how he loved her.

But in the palace of the king, everyone was stirring.

"So you're looking for a king?" Herod asked his visitors.

"Yes," one of them answered. "The newborn King of the Jews."

Herod wanted to say it. He really wanted to let them know. "I am the King of the Jews!" But he had to control himself – he knew it – if he was to discover what these foreigners were up to.

"We have followed a star," explained another visitor, "all the way from Babylon. It led us here, to Judea, and we thought you, of all people, might be able to tell us exactly where to find this new king."

49

"And why would you want to find him?" asked Herod suspiciously.

"Why, so we could honour him with the gifts we have brought," the visitor answered.

"So could you tell us, please," added a third visitor. "Even a hint would help – a prophecy, perhaps, from one of your holy books."

"Stars and prophecies," thought Herod. "Stars and prophecies and ghosts. Why won't they leave me alone?" And for an instant, he considered sending these star-gazers away. But, what if...? What if there really was a king, a baby king, out there? A king who would one day wrest the throne from him. Then he needed to know about it. He needed to find it. And he needed, most of all, to destroy it – before it had the chance to destroy him!

And so Herod shouted, "Fetch the priests. No, the chief priests! And the scribes, as well. Fetch anyone who can help us find this king!"

The night was a dark-blue blanket. It lay over the hills and the shepherds and their sheep. And over the carpenter and his family, as they prepared at last to go to sleep.

But in the palace of the king, everyone was awake. Wide awake!

Herod snapped his fingers. "Hurry!" he commanded. "You are the experts in these things, so tell me. Where do the prophets say the King of the Jews will be born?"

"Well, if it's the Messiah you mean," answered one of the priests, "then the prophets are very clear."

"Bethlehem," replied another priest, "according to the words of the prophet Micah."

"Excellent!" Herod smiled. "Now you may go."

"But if I may," asked one of the chief priests, "Why is your Majesty suddenly interested in this?"

"I have my reasons," growled the king. "Now, as I said, you may go." And the priests hurried off into the night.

As soon as the priests had gone, Herod sent for the visitors. "Tell me again," he said. "You have been following this star for how long?"

"Two years, your Majesty," answered one of the visitors.

Herod nodded his head, "And so that would make this new king how old?"

"No more than two years," the visitors explained.

"I see," Herod nodded again. "Well, I have good news for you. My priests tell me that Bethlehem is the town you're looking for. It's not far from here." And then, trying hard to look as innocent as possible, he added, "Perhaps you could do me a favour once you get there. I, too, would like to honour this new king. So when you have found him, could you come and tell me exactly where he is?"

The night was bright with stars. But one star shone brightest of all. It hovered above the house of the carpenter and his family. It waited for the star-gazers, just as it had shown them the way. And then it watched as they knocked on the door, and were greeted by the sleepy carpenter, and went in to worship the child. And when they had offered their gifts and walked out of the house again, it winked goodbye and joined its brothers in the sky.

In the house of Herod, however, the king sat alone. Alone with his suspicions and fears. Alone with the ghosts.

"Yes, yes," he muttered, "I know what you're thinking. To make a ghost of a child is the greatest evil of all. But I can't take the chance, don't you see? No, I'm not worried about him growing up and taking my place. I'll have joined your company by then. What worries me is what might happen here and now. What if he has some legitimate claim to the throne? Or what if – God forbid! – he really is the Messiah? All my enemies would need to do is get hold of that child and use him against me. Moan all you want. Rustle the tapestries. Wail through the walls. Do what you will to frighten me. But I will not be moved from my course. When the star-gazers return, the child will die. And then he will be yours to deal with."

The night crept over the star-gazers and swallowed them in sleep. They dreamed of shiny things – of stars and gold and bright perfume bottles. And then, something brighter still invaded their dreams – something shinier than their guiding star, purer than their golden gifts, and sweeter-smelling than all their balms and ointments. And they knew it could only be a messenger from God.

"Do not return to Herod," the messenger warned them. "For he is a wicked man, and he means to kill the boy. Sneak out of this country. Take another route home. And take the secret of the child with you."

The star-gazers left at once. And Herod awoke with a start – roused by darker spirits, perhaps – and called for his guard.

"There is something wrong," he said. "Go to Bethlehem immediately, and bring me the visitors from the east."

When the soldiers returned with news that the visitors had gone, Herod was not surprised. And he was not worried, either. For he had already devised a cruel alternative. So cruel that the soldiers, themselves, could hardly keep from weeping.

"You will kill every boy in Bethlehem," he ordered. "Every boy two years old or younger. You will be quick. You will be thorough. And you will show no mercy. This child will not escape me!"

As soon as the soldiers departed, the ghosts surrounded Herod. They clawed at his mind and tore at his heart. They raced around inside his head. And even as their numbers grew – child by murdered child – he would not be moved. Instead, he answered their dying screams with madman cries of his own: "I am the King of the Jews! I am Herod the Great! And no one will take my throne from me!"

But as those cries echoed around his dark and ghostly bedchamber, the angels went to work again – warning the carpenter and his family and guarding them as they crept off safely and escaped into the night.

Questions

1. I have portrayed Herod in a specific way – a man surrounded by ghosts. In what other ways might I have portrayed him?

2. "Ghosts" are a familiar way of dramatizing guilt (think Scrooge here, while we're considering Christmas stories!). Are you ever troubled by "ghosts"? What do you do to chase them away?

3. Compare and contrast angels and ghosts.

Consolation

(Luke 2:21–32)

Introduction

Sometimes things come up in the Bible and you say to yourself, "How did that work? What was that like?" Simeon's story is one of those times. It's all pure speculation, of course – how he felt, how he dealt with his impending/ not-impending death. And there is no suggestion that seeing the Messiah meant that he would drop over dead right there and then. Still, it's an interesting promise and gets you thinking. Well, it got me thinking, anyway, and this little piece was the result.

TELLING TIPS: Another one to tell on your own.

I wonder how Simeon waited.

The promise was clear enough: "You will not die until you have seen the Messiah."

But how did he handle that promise? That's what I want to know. Was he like an elderly friend who once told me she could not understand why the Lord had not yet taken her. No, I suppose, for he knew why he was still alive. But were there moments – moments when he wondered why the Messiah had not yet come? Moments when he wondered what God was waiting for? Exhausted moments. Moments of frustration. Moments aching with pain, and more. Moments when he missed his nearest and dearest. Moments when he wondered, "Why not today?"

Or did he wait in dread? Was the promise a kind of two-edged guarantee of immortality? Was he like the man who dreams of his own demise and then fears no danger except those circumstances which the dream revealed? Did he sigh a relieved sigh and crack a little smile at the end of each day – when the temple courts had cleared? "Perhaps I'll visit the park tomorrow. Feed the birds. Visit the grandchildren – one last time." For every time was conceivably that last time – if the right man and the right woman and the right child wandered into the temple precincts.

"The child is destined to cause the rise and fall of many in Israel." That's what he said to Mary. And even if that prophecy had never come true for anyone else, it surely was true for him.

The child comes. He falls. Well, "is dismissed" is how he puts it.

No child? He rises for one more day.

Yes, I know, all of this is true for each of us, as well. But to have it spelled out, so clearly. The sign. The moment. The event. Surely that must make a difference.

Or have I missed the point completely, because I have tried to put myself in his worn sandals and aching feet, and not allowed him to be himself?

"Righteous and devout." That's how the passage describes him. "A servant" is how he describes himself. So is it possible that there was something more at work than just his impatience or his dread? Is it possible that, at the heart of his experience, there was simply the willingness to let God be in charge, and choose his own timing, as long as meeting the Messiah was at the end of it?

And in that – in theory – is there really any difference between us at all?

I wonder how Simeon waited.

I wonder if I can wait that way, too.

Questions

1. How would you have felt if you had been in Simeon's sandals?

2. How would that position have changed the way you lived each day?

3. Has God ever asked you to do something that seemed a little strange, a little difficult, a little like what Simeon faced?

A Trip to the Temple

(Luke 2:41–50)

Introduction

The trick with these rhyming readings is to get enough rhymes to make them work. I started this one late at night, did really well until the end, and then got stuck. Thus "off-piste"! Yeah, it's a stretch – but it's growing on me.

> **TELLING TIPS: See "Mary Meets an Angel" (above) for suggestions on how best to do this kind of reading.**

Jesus and his parents went up to Jerusalem,
Jesus and his parents went up to Jerusalem,
Jesus and his parents went up to Jerusalem,
Went up for the Passover Feast.
(Pretend to eat, gobble up, feast.)
Went up for the Passover Feast.
Went up for the Passover Feast.

When the feast was finished, they set off for their home,
When the feast was finished, they set off for their home,
When the feast was finished, they set off for their home,
Ninety miles away from the south-east.
(Do a compass-y motion with body and arm, pointing roughly in a south-easterly direction.)
Ninety miles away from the southeast.
Ninety miles away from the southeast.

Jesus' parents thought their boy was walking with his friends.
Jesus' parents thought their boy was walking with his friends.

Jesus' parents thought their boy was walking with his friends.
They didn't realize that their family had decreased.
(Bring hands together to show something shrinking.)
They didn't realize that their family had decreased.
They didn't realize that their family had decreased.

When they saw their son was missing, they headed back at once,
When they saw their son was missing, they headed back at once,
When they saw their son was missing, they headed back at once,
Hoping that their boy was not deceased.
(Make a hands-around-throat motion, or head lolling to one side.)
Hoping that their boy was not deceased.
Hoping that their boy was not deceased.

After three long days they found him, sitting in the temple,
After three long days they found him, sitting in the temple,
After three long days they found him, sitting in the temple,
Talking with the teachers and the priests.
(Hands folded.)
Talking with the teachers and the priests.
Talking with the teachers and the priests.

Everyone who heard him was astonished by his words,
Everyone who heard him was astonished by his words,
Everyone who heard him was astonished by his words,
And wondered how his knowledge had increased.
(Hands growing apart – opposite of decrease motion.)
And wondered how his knowledge had increased.
And wondered how his knowledge had increased.

But his mum, being a mum, did the mum thing and she said,
But his mum, being a mum, did the mum thing and she said,
But his mum, being a mum, did the mum thing and she said,
"We were worried, son. You could have called, at least!"
(Pretend phone-call motion.)
"We were worried, son. You could have called, at least!"
"We were worried, son. You could have called, at least!"

"This is my Father's house," Jesus told her with a smile.
"This is my Father's house," Jesus told her with a smile.
"This is my Father's house," Jesus told her with a smile.
"I'm where I'm s'pposed to be, I'm not off-piste."
(Skiing motion.)
"I'm where I'm s'pposed to be, I'm not off-piste."
"I'm where I'm s'pposed to be, I'm not off-piste."

So they headed off for Nazareth, together once again,
So they headed off for Nazareth, together once again,
So they headed off for Nazareth, together once again,
Back home from the Passover Feast.
(Repeat first motion.)
Back home from the Passover Feast.
Back home from the Passover Feast.

Questions

1. How could Jesus' parents have lost track of him?

2. How would you have reacted if you had made the discovery they did? I mean, both the "missing" bit and the "talking with the teachers" bit.

3. So is Jesus being just a bit cheeky to his mum here? How do you read his response?

The Tempter's Tale

(Luke 4:1–13)

Introduction

My son is a fan of martial arts films – all that high-kicking, kung fu-fighting stuff. In every one of those films, right at the end, there is always the Big Confrontation between the good guy and the bad guy (except for *Zatoichi*, where, strangely, there is a big dance number). But before that – usually quite early in the film – there is another battle, a smaller battle, where the good guy and the bad guy discover each other's strengths and weaknesses. That's the battle I have chosen to deal with in this story. Not the Big Confrontation between Jesus and the devil – the one at the end of the story where the devil's triumph on the cross is snatched away three days later. The one where he is left holding nothing but an empty tomb.

No, this is the earlier battle, the quiet one in the desert, where they looked at each other face to face and tested each other's will.

TELLING TIPS: One to read/tell on your own.

He scratched at the ground with his cracked, dry fingers. He scratched at the dirt and the pebbles and the sand. He scratched out shapes and circles and lines. He was doodling. He was thinking. He was praying. He was hungry.

For forty days he had fasted. Forty days without food. Forty days in the desert. Forty days alone. Forty days to chart the course his life would take. Forty days to consider what it meant to be the Saviour of the world!

Fasting clears the head, he had been taught. Fasting helps you see things more clearly. Fasting brings you closer to God. And all these things had proved true. But fasting also makes you sick with hunger – aching, gnawing, belly-screaming hunger! And maybe that was why he was suddenly no longer alone.

His companion was handsome, confident, persuasive, poised. And his suggestions seemed not only sensible, but kind:

"If you're hungry, why not eat?"

"If you're the Saviour of the world, why not use your power?"

"If there are stones, why not turn them into bread?"

Jesus considered the words – considered them carefully. And he considered the face of his companion, as well. The smile could not have been more genuine, the eyes more sincere. But the words – the words were lies. They were poison.

"There are more important things than bread," Jesus replied. "That's what the Scriptures say. There is God, and all that he wants to give us. So if doing without bread helps me to get closer to him, then I am quite happy to go hungry."

"The Scriptures," his companion nodded. "Of course. There is a great deal of truth in them, isn't there? Why, just the other day, I read this remarkable passage about the angels. Shall I tell you about it?"

Jesus just shrugged. He suspected that it would have been pointless to say no. He had it on good authority that his companion was nothing if not persistent.

He sat down beside Jesus and scratched some lines of his own in the sand.

"Imagine this," he said, tracing out a perfect sketch of a tall and majestic building. "The Temple in Jerusalem. Do you see it? And here, at the top of the very tallest tower, someone who wants attention. Someone who needs to gather a crowd. Someone who wants to demonstrate God's power. Someone like you, maybe."

He sketched a tiny figure at the top of the tower, and then drew a long line down to the ground below.

"Now suppose this someone was to leap from the Temple top. Do you know what the Scriptures say would happen? The Scriptures say that if that someone was someone special – God's own Son, perhaps – then the angels would come to his rescue before his feet ever touched the ground!"

Jesus nodded and traced out the shape of a heart.

"Yes, they do," he agreed. "But the Scriptures also say that God loves us. That we should trust that love. And that it would be wrong to put ourselves in foolish and dangerous places to put that love to the test."

"But what about your mission?" asked the companion, more confident than ever. "Surely, saving the world is your life's work. And if it's the world you want, then I am the one to give it to you."

He stood up. He waved wide his arms. And a hot wind swept up a desert full of drawings. Armies and palaces. Treasures and thrones. All that anyone could ever want sprang up before Jesus and stood glittering and golden against the purple sundown sky. And all the while, his companion's words echoed in his ears:

"All of this I will give you if you will bow down and worship me!"

But Jesus did not move. For there were other words, as well. Words that he knew from his childhood and before. And these were the words he whispered as he drew one last shape on the ground.

"I will worship the Lord my God and him alone will I serve."

Jesus looked up. The vision was gone, and so was the smile on his companion's face.

"I don't understand," he said. "I offer you the world and you draw an X through it?"

"Not an X," said Jesus. "A cross." And that was when he noticed the blood on his companion's head.

"You're hurt," said Jesus.

"It's nothing," muttered his companion.

But as they stared at each other, both of them remembered one more scripture – an old promise about a child and a battle and a crushing blow to a serpent's head.

"I will be back," said the companion.

"I will be waiting," said Jesus.

And suddenly he was alone again. Considering the course of his life. Thinking. Praying. Doodling. So he scratched at the ground with his cracked, dry finger. He scratched a circle beside the cross.

The shape of the sun as it set?

The whole of the moon as it rose?

Or the mouth of an empty tomb?

Questions

1. Why do you think the devil chose those three temptations in particular?

2. What three temptations might he choose for you? Where would your areas of weakness lie?

3. Does the devil still twist Scripture to entice people? List some examples.

Hometown Boy

(Luke 4:14–30)

Introduction

Having preached in my hometown church, I think I have some sympathy both for what Jesus had to deal with and also for the woman in this story. (The other voice is most definitely a woman – older, a widow – sitting in the back of the room where she can't quite see or hear.) The desire is to wish the best for the hometown boy, to say you "knew him when…" if he's doing well. And all of that comes up in this piece. I read somewhere that there were probably no more than 100–120 people living in Nazareth at that time, so it wasn't just some people who knew the hometown boy, it was probably everybody. That makes this whole event even more extraordinary, and the woman's reaction even more amusing!

TELLING TIPS: You'll need one person to read the Bible passage in a straightforward way, and another person to play the part of the woman who is whispering (loudly) to the woman sitting next to her.

Jesus returned to Galilee in the power of the Spirit, and news about him spread through the whole countryside. He taught in their synagogues and everyone praised him.

He went to Nazareth, where he had been brought up, and on the Sabbath day he went into the synagogue, as was his custom. And he stood up to read.

"Ooh, look! Isn't that Jesus – Joseph and Mary's son?"

The scroll of the prophet Isaiah was handed to him.

"He looks good, doesn't he? I like what he's done with his hair!"

Unrolling it, he found the place and began to read.

"He played with my boys, you know – Abraham, Samuel and little Judas."

"The Spirit of the Lord is on me..."

"Always creeping up and tripping him, he was. Sneaky little beggar, my Judas."

"Because he has anointed me to preach good news to the poor..."

"We had him for dinner on more than one occasion."

"He has sent me to proclaim freedom for the prisoners..."

"Absolutely adored my baked beans. But they didn't agree with him, poor boy."

"And recovery of sight for the blind..."

"'You can make those noises in a carpenter's shop,' I'd say, 'but not in this house!'"

"To release the oppressed..."

"Has a clear speaking voice, doesn't he?"

"To proclaim the year of the Lord's favour."

"You don't have to strain to hear – not like some I could mention."

Then he rolled up the scroll, gave it back to the attendant and sat down.

"And look at that body language. Poised. Confident. He'll go far."

The eyes of everyone in the synagogue were fastened on him.

"I bet his mother's pleased."

And he began by saying, "Today this scripture is fulfilled in your hearing."

"That was nice, wasn't it? A lovely sentiment."

All spoke well of him and were amazed at the gracious words that came from his lips.

"So well spoken. Such gracious words. Is he wearing a little gloss on his lips?"

"But isn't this Joseph's son?" they asked.

"Actually, I've heard rumours about that. But I'll say no more."

Jesus said to them, "Surely you will quote this proverb to me, 'Physician, heal yourself.'"

"This is so nice, isn't it?"

"'Do here in your hometown what we have heard you did in Capernaum.'"

"Hometown boy, reading and preaching. Brings a tear to the eye, doesn't it?"

"I tell you the truth," he continued, "no prophet is accepted in his hometown."

"Somebody you know. Somebody you can trust. Somebody who won't rock the boat."

"I assure you, there were many widows in Israel in Elijah's time, when the sky was shut for three and a half years and there was a severe famine throughout the land. Yet Elijah was not sent to any of them, but to a gentile widow in Zarephath in the region of Sidon."

"Gentle Jesus, meek and mild. We used to call him that, you know. He was lovely!"

"And there were many in Israel with leprosy in the time of Elisha the prophet, yet not one of them was cleansed – only Naaman the Syrian – the gentile."

"No trouble. No trouble at all."

All the people in the synagogue were furious when they heard this.

"It's getting a little noisy in here. Are we finished already?"

They got up...

"Where's everyone going? His mother's planned a little reception, of course!"

... drove him out of the town and took him to the brow of the hill on which the town was built in order to throw him down the cliff.

"To the cliffside, you say? Is that where we're going? For a little picnic, I imagine."

But he walked right through the crowd and went on his way.

"I don't know about you, but I think it's lovely to see a hometown boy do well!"

Questions

1. Like the woman in the story, people often place on Jesus the image they have of him, regardless of any evidence to the contrary. Can you cite any examples of how that happens today?

2. How might you react if a young minister who had come from your church returned to say that he was God's special prophet? What actions might be taken?

3. The woman calls him "Gentle Jesus, meek and mild." Can you cite any biblical references to support that view? To contradict it?

A Day at the Seaside on the Magic Roundabout

(Luke 5:1–11)

Introduction

Here's another one of those three-line-rhyming retellings. Apologies to mushy pea enthusiasts. And yes, I know that the *Magic Roundabout* reference is anachronistic, but I have found that a little anachronism here and there keeps these stories fresh and interesting for adults as well as children.

> **TELLING TIPS: See "Mary Meets an Angel" (above) for suggestions on how to tell this kind of story.**

Jesus was talking to a crowd down by the sea,
Jesus was talking to a crowd down by the sea,
Jesus was talking to a crowd down by the sea,
Sitting on the shores of Galilee.
(Make shape of lake with hands.)
Sitting on the shores of Galilee.
Sitting on the shores of Galilee.

"The crowd's too big," he said to Peter, "could I borrow your boat?"
"The crowd's too big," he said to Peter, "could I borrow your boat?"
"The crowd's too big," he said to Peter, "could I borrow your boat?"
And he taught them all a-floating on the sea.
(Make waving, sea motion.)
And he taught them all a-floating on the sea.
And he taught them all a-floating on the sea.

"Let's go fishing," said Jesus, when the talking was done.
"Let's go fishing," said Jesus, when the talking was done.
"Let's go fishing," said Jesus, when the talking was done.
"I'm feeling peckish, I need something for my tea."
(Pretend to sip cup of tea.)
"I'm feeling peckish, I need something for my tea."
"I'm feeling peckish, I need something for my tea."

"We've caught nothing all day," said Peter with a sigh.
"We've caught nothing all day," said Peter with a sigh.
"We've caught nothing all day," said Peter with a sigh.
"We'll have no fish with our chips and mushy peas."
(Look in pretend pot, go icck!)
"We'll have no fish with our chips and mushy peas."
"We'll have no fish with our chips and mushy peas."

"Trust me," said Jesus, "throw your nets out over there.
"Trust me," said Jesus, "throw your nets out over there.
"Trust me," said Jesus, "throw your nets out over there.
I think you'll be surprised by what you see."
(Hold hand over eyes in looking motion.)
I think you'll be surprised by what you see."
I think you'll be surprised by what you see."

So Peter trusted Jesus, threw his nets out over there,
So Peter trusted Jesus, threw his nets out over there,
So Peter trusted Jesus, threw his nets out over there,
And had a catch with a capital C.
(Make 'C' with fingers.)
And had a catch with a capital C.
And had a catch with a capital C.

There were so many fish, he couldn't pull them all in.
There were so many fish, he couldn't pull them all in.
There were so many fish, he couldn't pull them all in.
"Help me, James and John, the sons of Zebedee!"
(Bounce and go "boing" like the Magic Roundabout *character.)*
"Help me, James and John, the sons of Zebedee!"

"Help me, James and John, the sons of Zebedee!"

Peter was astonished and he fell to the floor.
Peter was astonished and he fell to the floor.
Peter was astonished and he fell to the floor.
"I'm not worthy, go away, I beg you, please!"
(Hands in praying position.)
"I'm not worthy, go away, I beg you, please!"
"I'm not worthy, go away, I beg you, please!"

"Get up," said Jesus, "I've got a job for you to do.
"Get up," said Jesus, "I've got a job for you to do.
"Get up," said Jesus, "I've got a job for you to do.
I don't want you trembling on your knees."
(Point to knees, wobble them.)
I don't want you trembling on your knees."
I don't want you trembling on your knees."

"You've been fishing for fish," Jesus said with a grin.
"You've been fishing for fish," Jesus said with a grin.
"You've been fishing for fish," Jesus said with a grin.
"You'll fish for men if you follow after me."
(Point to self.)
"You'll fish for men if you follow after me."
"You'll fish for men if you follow after me."

So Peter got up and followed after Jesus,
So Peter got up and followed after Jesus,
So Peter got up and followed after Jesus,
And so did the sons of Zebedee.
(Repeat earlier motion.)
And so did the sons of Zebedee.
They left their nets on the shores of Galilee.
(Repeat earlier motion.)

Questions

1. I read somewhere that Peter and the other disciples were probably no older than nineteen or twenty. How does that affect the way you see them? The way you see this story?

2. What might your reaction have been, had someone who knew nothing about your profession tried to tell you how to do your job? Particularly a member of the clergy. Why do you think Peter went along with what Jesus said?

3. What do you think it means to "fish for men"?

Peterfish Song

(Luke 5:1–11)

Introduction

Here's another song. You could make up your own tune, or listen to a clip of the tune that I use on my website (www.kregel.com/bobhartman). As you will see, it's a bit of a sea shanty – fitting, I think, given the nautical theme. The "Arrr!" is a pirate-y, West Country sort of thing, courtesy of my time in Wiltshire. And the chorus is a gentle nod to Dr Seuss.

TELLING TIPS: I usually teach the chorus to the crowd and do the verses myself. There are a few simple actions that make the chorus easier to learn:

"One fish" *(hold up one finger – no, not fish fingers!)*
"two fish" *(hold up two fingers)*
"me fish" *(point to self)*
"you've been" *(point to someone else)*
"Fishing for fish, Peter my friend" *(casting, reeling motion)*

Then repeat the motions in the second half of the chorus. If you like, you can put one hand over one eye – like a patch.

Peter went out on the sea one day
But all of the fishes went swimming away.
"Peter," said Jesus, "can I borrow your boat?
It's no use to you anyway,
Hey, it's no use to you anyway!"

One fish, two fish, me fish, you've been
Fishing for fish, Peter my friend.
One fish, two fish, me fish, you fish,
Now you'll be fishing for men, (Arrr!)
Now you'll be fishing for men.

"Peter," said Jesus, "I've got an idea.
Row out to deep water, anywhere far or near.
Lower your nets off the side of the boat.
There's something I need to make clear,
Hey, there's something I need to make clear."

Chorus

Peter dropped anchor and lowered his nets.
They filled up so fast he broke out in a sweat.
His friends James and John floated by to assist.
"That's the biggest catch that you've caught yet,
Hey, the biggest catch that you've caught yet!"

Chorus

"It's all down to Jesus. It's him and not me.
He's special," said Peter, as he fell to his knees.
"Get up," said Jesus, "and please don't be scared.
I want you to come follow me,
Hey, I want you to come follow me!"

Chorus

Questions

See the previous story.

A Roof Story

(Luke 5:17–26)

Introduction

This is one of my favourite New Testament stories, one which I have already told in a number of different ways. I was really pleased to find enough rhymes to tell it this way, as well!

We lived in Leicestershire for eight years, by the way, and I still haven't found a cheddar that beats Leicester Red.

> **TELLING TIPS: See "Mary Meets an Angel" (above) for suggestions on telling this kind of story.**

Jesus was teaching in a house, one day.
Jesus was teaching in a house, one day.
Jesus was teaching in a house, one day.
It was crowded! It was packed! It was a squeeze!
(Make squeezed motion – look like you're squeezed.)
It was crowded! It was packed! It was a squeeze!
It was crowded! It was packed! It was a squeeze!

All of a sudden, bits of roof fell in!
All of a sudden, bits of roof fell in!
All of a sudden, bits of roof fell in!
"Is it me?" said Jesus. "Do you feel a breeze?"
(Wave hand like breeze.)
"Is it me?" said Jesus. "Do you feel a breeze?"
"Is it me?" said Jesus. "Do you feel a breeze?"

"We're sorry," said the men who had torn the roof apart.
"We're sorry," said the men who had torn the roof apart.
"We're sorry," said the men who had torn the roof apart.
"Our friend is paralyzed. Could you help him, please?"
(Make pleading, praying motion with hands.)
"Our friend is paralyzed. Could you help him, please?"
"Our friend is paralyzed. Could you help him, please?"

So they lowered the man, on a mat, into the room,
So they lowered the man, on a mat, into the room,
So they lowered the man, on a mat, into the room,
Hanging from the roof like chimpanzees.
(Make monkey sounds and motions.)
Hanging from the roof like chimpanzees.
Hanging from the roof like chimpanzees.

"Your sins are forgiven," said Jesus to the man.
"Your sins are forgiven," said Jesus to the man.
"Your sins are forgiven," said Jesus to the man.
"I'm serious. It's not some kind of wheeze."
(Make a little heh-heh sound – or wheeze.)
"I'm serious. It's not some kind of wheeze."
"I'm serious. It's not some kind of wheeze."

"Only God can do that!" the religious leaders fumed.
"Only God can do that!" the religious leaders fumed.
"Only God can do that!" the religious leaders fumed.
And their faces turned red as Leicester cheese.
(Do that Wallace and Gromit thing with your fingers when you say, in a Wallace-y way, "Cheese".)
And their faces turned red as Leicester cheese.
And their faces turned red as Leicester cheese.

"What is harder?" asked Jesus, a twinkle in his eye.
"What is harder?" asked Jesus, a twinkle in his eye.
"What is harder?" asked Jesus, a twinkle in his eye.

"To forgive a man's sin or fix his knees?"
(Point to knees.)
"To forgive a man's sin or fix his knees?"
"To forgive a man's sin or fix his knees?"

"To prove I have authority and pow'r to do the first,
"To prove I have authority and pow'r to do the first,
"To prove I have authority and pow'r to do the first,
I'll do the second," Jesus grinned, "with ease!"
(Hands behind head, smile – like you're resting.)
I'll do the second," Jesus grinned, "with ease!"
I'll do the second," Jesus grinned, "with ease!"

"Get up. Go home!" said Jesus to the man.
"Get up. Go home!" said Jesus to the man.
"Get up. Go home!" said Jesus to the man.
And he stood up and walked – just like John Cleese!
(That's right – do something from the Ministry of Silly Walks!)
And he stood up and walked – just like John Cleese!
And he stood up and walked – just like John Cleese!

The crowd praised God. They were in awe of Jesus.
The crowd praised God. They were in awe of Jesus.
The crowd praised God. They were in awe of Jesus.
But his enemies were still red as Leicester cheese.
(Repeat Wallace motion.)
But his enemies were still red as Leicester cheese.
But his enemies were still red as Leicester cheese.

Questions

1. Put yourself in the place of the man who owned the house. Your reaction?

2. What about the four friends? How might they have felt as they were tearing up the roof? At the end of the story?

3. And why were the religious leaders so upset?

Poor, Hungry, Sad, and Unpopular

(Luke 6:20–26)

Introduction

It was the "Whoah/Woe" thing that started this one off. And the "Bless" just followed along. And because this version of the beatitudes is less familiar than the one from Matthew, it was easier to "play" with.

> **TELLING TIPS:** After the "Blessed" lines, look at the person next to you, and say "Bless!" (Maybe even put your arm around their shoulder!)
>
> After the "Woe" lines, pull on imaginary reins, like you are slowing down a horse, and say "Whoah!" Explain that putting a stop to the kind of life that has no need for God is at the heart of both "Woe" and "Whoah!"

Are you poor? Then you are blessed, *(Bless!)*
For God will give you his kingdom.

Are you hungry? Then you are blessed, *(Bless!)*
For God will fill you up.

Are you weeping? Then you are blessed, *(Bless!)*
For God will bring a smile to your face.

Are you hated, excluded, rejected, persecuted? Then you are blessed,
  (Bless!)
Because that's how God's messengers are always treated. And they get
  God's reward!

Or are you wealthy? Then woe, *(Whoah!)*
You have all the comfort you're going to get.

Are you full? Then woe, *(Whoah!)*
For you will feel the pangs of hunger.

Are you laughing? Then woe, *(Whoah!)*
Tears will flow from your eyes.

Are you popular? Then woe, *(Whoah!)*
So were the false prophets, who had no word from God.

So God wants us poor, hungry, sad and unpopular? (a bit like school!)
Looks like it. Because then and only then do we reach out in need for
  him.
And then, and only then, do we get blessed. *(Bless!)*

Questions

1. Does God really want us to be poor, hungry, sad and unpopular?

2. This is a real reversal of what we generally consider success to be. But what if you are successful? Is that necessarily a bad thing?

3. Which of these woes, in particular, keeps you from trusting in God?

What Would Jesus Drive?

(Matthew 5:29–30)

Introduction

I had this idea for a book, a couple of years ago, that was inspired by a website run by a group of Christians who were particularly concerned about the environment. Playing with the good ol' WWJD bracelet thing, they came up with the title *What Would Jesus Drive?* for their site.

Being a lifelong motor junkie, however, I immediately imagined a kind of Holy Top Gear, where automotive reviews and theology would collide at some strange junction. Jeremiah Clarkson. St James May. That sort of thing.

The publishers said 'no'. Who could blame them? But there was still this sample piece, revving away among my other documents, desperate to spin its wheels and launch itself onto a public highway.

So here it is. At last. You might want to put the Allman Brothers' "Jessica" on before you read it. Then "Shine, Jesus Shine". Just to get in the mood. And read Matthew 5:29–30.

TELLING TIPS: See above.

There are some people you can't help but envy.

This is, of course, in clear violation of the tenth commandment. Or at least it was until a Channel Four poll decided that, in the twenty-first century, commandment number ten really had no right to be in the list at all. It was replaced, I think, by something much more trendy like "Love yourself" or "Be kind to foxes" or "Try hard not to wear plaid".

In my case, I envy my brother-in-law, Brian. Why? Purely and simply because he's so dog-gone clever!

He's got a degree in physics and spends most of his time writing computer software for a major American university. But he's also got a degree in music – the pipe organ, specifically. And, to top it off, he can build just about anything he sets his mind to.

Ten years ago, when he and I decided to form a folk band, Bri not only taught himself to play the hammered dulcimer, he also built one from scratch and composed a collection of tunes to perform on it. In his spare time, of course.

It may come as no surprise, then, to discover that Brian's favourite car manufacturer is Honda. I would like to say that he has garages full of the things, but the fact of the matter is that, over the years, he has owned just a few. Because that's the reality of life for Honda drivers.

Fiat drivers and Alfa drivers and Renault drivers have garages full of their favourite vehicles, because they are constantly borrowing bits off them to keep their car of choice on the road. But Honda drivers need just one Honda at a time. Because Hondas don't break down.

That is why Honda's image in the UK has always been associated with grey-haired motorists and the clogging up of A-roads. Experience accompanies those grey hairs, and experience suggests that a reliable vehicle that delivers on its promises and gets you where you're going on time is better than one that doesn't. (It's why you see fewer and fewer pensioners on the trains, for example. Well, that, and the fact that it now costs a week's pension to make the average rail journey.)

But while Honda may well be the car of choice in the average UK rest home car park, in the rest of the world, and certainly in the opinion of my brother-in-law Brian, it is recognized for exactly what it is – one of the few automotive manufacturing companies that has consistently combined superb engineering design, technical innovation, and reliability. And for that, Honda is envied.

Forgetting about their ground-breaking motorcycles, just think for a moment about their cars. In the sixties, while the average British sports car was being tugged around by antediluvian overhead valves and pushrods, Honda's S-800 roadsters and coupés were quite literally buzzing up and down our roads to the song of roller-bearing overhead camshafts spinning at 7,000 revolutions per minute.

In the seventies, while most British cars were spewing forth clouds of damaging hydrocarbons, Honda Civics were cleaning up both their act and our air with CVCC engines, developed for an American market that was moving rapidly towards catalytic converters and unleaded fuel.

And in the eighties, while most motorists could only dream of a time when they could enjoy supercar power and handling at an affordable price, Honda went and built the NSX, and made that dream a reality. I could go on: the Civic Type R, the S-2000, the hybrid Insight, Variable Valve Timing Technology, even the packaging miracle that is the Jazz super-mini. But what I really want to talk about is the Honda Accord Diesel. Because that is the car my brother-in-law Brian thinks that Jesus would drive.

I collected the graphite pearl Accord at my local Honda dealership on the edge of Chippenham, and headed down the A420 towards Bristol.

The first thing I noticed was the noise – or rather, the lack of it. My regular drive is a K-Reg Citroen BX Diesel. In its time, the 1.9 diesel was state-of-the-art, and the fleet of elderly BX's and ZX's still chugging up and down Britain's highways is a testament to that engine's durability and excellent fuel economy. But its time was a long time ago – and a lot has changed. Shakespear's Sister on a Walkman, then. Scissor Sisters on an iPod®, now. And there was a different tune coming from under the bonnet of the Accord, as well.

On start-up, my BX sounds a bit like Bob Dylan. With a sore throat. On a bad day. Gargling marbles. But the Accord? The Accord is Joss Stone. Yeah, there's still a little grittiness there. But it's a smooth and soulful sound you wouldn't mind listening to over the next 300 miles or so.

So with Joss Stone under the bonnet (and, coincidentally, on the standard in-dash six-CD changer, as well), I eventually turned off the A420, and headed for Castle Combe. The track was closed, but I have no doubt that the Accord would have acquitted itself well. Unlike some laggy turbo diesels, this engine's power is always "right there" – 138 horsepower and 250 pounds of torque, to be precise. The handling is note-perfect, the steering just right, and the ride comfortable, if a little firm. It's an almost perfect combination that makes a confident and assured driver out of anyone gripping the leather-clad wheel. And if I had run into trouble, there was always standard ABS, EBD, and six airbags to help me out.

The village of Castle Combe lies beyond the track, nestled in the valley below. It's one of those chocolate-box places where only the well-heeled can afford to purchase the thatched-roof confectionery containers on offer. I would have looked well and truly out of place in my BX (or been mistaken for one of the local tradesmen), but the Accord fitted in nicely with the pik'n'mix of Audis, Beemers and Mercs scattered around the village. Or at least it did to my eyes. The deep-grey pearl paintwork and tasteful touches of chrome were classy. And the leather seats, soft mouldings, and first-class build quality carried the theme inside. But I suspect that the inhabitants of the village would have looked no further than the H-shaped badge on the bonnet and dismissed it straight away. Another misguided victory for British badge snobbery.

I have always found this attitude hard to understand. Japanese cars are, by almost every measure, the best-built vehicles in the world. But in nearly every British review of a Japanese car that I have ever read, there is inevitably a "but". Well built, yes. Reliable, yes. But "bland", "soul-less", "an appliance". Or in one case, when the styling was that bit more adventurous – "tries too hard". Tries too hard? What does that mean, exactly? It means that the reviewer couldn't find anything else to criticize, that's what it means.

My favourite, of course, is "It's just a mini-cab" – usually in reference to any older Nissan, Toyota, or Honda saloon. But how is this a criticism? Cabbies need a vehicle that is comfortable, economical, reliable, and good to drive. Isn't that what everyone is looking for? And don't cab drivers in many parts of the world drive Mercedes? How can that be bad company?

Of course, the irony is that Mercedes build quality has declined precipitously of late. And if it's not exactly "bad company", the average Mercedes is definitely nowhere near so responsible as it used to be. But British badge snobs still swoon at the site of anything Teutonic, regardless of every bit of objective evidence to the contrary. And this has been going on for ages. Drive any mid- to late-nineties Golf, and then climb into a corresponding Civic. I guarantee you that you will find the Golf heavy, slow, soggy round the corners, and not particularly well built. The Civic, however, will be agile, quick, and last forever. Which one holds its value best? The one with the Führer's People-Wagon badge on it, of course!

And speaking of the Führer, I have an uncle who was in the war and who refuses to drive anything German, Japanese, or Italian. But that is obviously not the root of the prejudice, here. No, in Britain, I think the prejudice stems from our old friend, commandment number ten – envy.

When Japanese cars were first introduced to these shores, they were dismissed outright. Go back and read those early reviews. But the foothold the Japanese carmakers established in the sixties eventually became a stranglehold, as their rise paralleled the decline of the home-grown motor industry. And today? Today we have Nissans built in

Sunderland, Hondas in Swindon, and Toyotas in Derbyshire. Today the British car industry *is* Japanese, and there would be hardly anything but niche models manufactured in the Land of Hope and Glory were it not for the Land of the Rising Sun. Yeah, I reckon it's all about envy.

Which brings me back to Brian. You see, as much as he likes the Accord diesel, the reason he thinks that Jesus would drive it has less to do with the car itself than it does with the promotional campaign that launched the car in the first place.

Perhaps you remember. The television advert was a cartoon, featuring lots of brightly coloured birds and woodland creatures and a hovering diesel engine. And the slogan? The slogan was simplicity itself, cleverly designed to stand out in sharp contrast to the happy animated background: "Hate Something. Change Something."

The reference was to Soichiro Honda, founder of the motor company that bears his name, and to his dislike (well, all right, then – his hatred) of the diesel engine. Slow, lumpy, thumpy, and heavy – it was the antithesis of the free-revving engines that made his reputation, and he was determined that a diesel should never find its way under the bonnet of one of his designs.

Soichiro Honda passed away in the early nineties, however, and the pressure to build a diesel engine, particularly for the European market, grew through the following decade until the Honda Motor Company could no longer afford to stay out of the diesel club. This did not mean, however, that they would ignore the wishes of their founder and driving spirit. No, as the slogan suggests, they were determined to use their founder's hatred of the diesel engine to transform the nature of the engine itself.

I could go into all the technical details, but it's far simpler to say that Honda's designers and engineers turned "slow, lumpy, thumpy, and heavy" into "quick, smooth, quiet, and light" and created what is regarded by many as the finest diesel engine in the world. On their very first try.

"Hate Something. Change Something." I think that Jesus might have used that slogan, too. Because it's just another way of saying, "Repent!" And more than that, it helps to explain some of the more "extreme"-sounding things that Jesus had to say about repentance. There was that whole business about plucking out one's eye and cutting off one's hand if one struggled with temptation – images redolent of a Tarantino film or an episode of *CSI*. And then there was his insistence that if his disciples were serious about following him, they would have to hate their mothers and fathers and brothers and sisters. It sounds like something right out of David Koresh's *Wacky Waco Training Manual*.

But "Hate Something. Change Something" helps to make sense of those pictures. Because change – real, true, lasting change – only happens when we are well and truly fed up with the way things are. And until we reach that point, we're only just going through the motions.

I can't tell you the number of diets I've started in my life. And if you're like the average person, then you have probably gone on a few, too. So you know how it is. There are the diets you start because someone has talked you into it, or because you feel guilty, or because it's January and everyone else is doing it. In my experience, those diets don't do anything but make me feel bad (and hungry).

But then there are the other diets – the ones that resulted from looking in the mirror and admitting that I really didn't want to see that any more. Or the ones that came about because I really didn't feel good and was desperate to feel better.

Do you see the difference? If you hate something, if you just can't stand it any more, then you're more likely to make the kind of change that lasts. This is obviously not just true of diets, but of lots of other areas of our lives, as well. Our selfishness, our pride, our bitterness, our pettiness. I could go on, and I'm sure you could, too.

So Jesus uses extreme language to make that clear. Real, lasting change doesn't result from deciding that I'll be a little nicer to the dog tomorrow. It comes about because I'm sick to death of living with myself the way I am and just have to learn to live my life a different way. I have to become a new person. I have to start all over – maybe even be born again.

So Jesus forgives, wipes the slate clean – so I can make a fresh start. And then he says, "Here's the Holy Spirit, God's force inside you, to give you the power to make those changes real." And "slow, lumpy, thumpy, and heavy" becomes "quick, smooth, quiet, and light".

Hate Something. Change Something. Guess I'll have to stop envying my brother-in-law, Brian. And coveting his Honda, as well.

Questions

1. So what do you think? Does it work? Do you want to read more? Address all correspondence to Lion Hudson...

2. Is this a fair description of repentance? Does it make what Jesus has to say any clearer?

3. What do you think Jesus would drive?

Rock and Sand

(Luke 6:46–49)

Introduction

It's interesting how stories change. When I first wrote *The Lion Storyteller Bible*, I told this story in one particular way. But as time passed, and I told it again and again, it morphed into something different – more like a poem, more like a song. So that's the version I'm using here.

TELLING TIPS: Choose a volunteer to play the rock. Ask him to take a wrestler's stance and growl every time you say "rock". Choose someone to stand beside him and play the house built on the rock (holding their hands over their head like a roof). Choose someone else to play the sand. They should sway and say "Shifty, shifty, shifty" every time you say "sand". Choose someone to play the house built on the sand, as well. Then choose someone (preferably an adult) to play the rain. Give them a loaded water pistol to spray on the respective pairs when the rain falls. Lead everyone else in being the wind and the waves.

There once was a man,
A wise and clever man,
Who decided to build himself a house.
So he found himself a rock,
A strong and mighty rock,
And on that rock he built himself a house.

And the wind blew,
And the waves rose,
And the rain fell down and down.

But because his house was built upon a rock,
It did not budge, not one bit.

There once was a man,
A not-so-clever man,
Who decided to build himself a house.
So he found himself some sand,
Some soft and shifty sand,
And on that sand he built himself a house.

And the wind blew,
And the waves rose,
And the rain fell down and down.

And because his house was built on the sand
The house fell down with a crash.

"My words," said Jesus, "are like that rock,
And if you build your life on them,
Then you will stand firm, as well,
Firm like the house on the rock."

Questions

1. Can you think of any "rock" examples in your own life – where you made a conscious decision to follow Jesus with regard to a specific issue/decision and you had a "firm" result?

2. Can you think of any "sandy" moments?

3. Are things always as straightforward as these two choices in your experience? Why or why not?

Having His Way

(Luke 7:1–10; Matthew 8:5–13)

Introduction

Sometimes it's a phrase that jumps out of a reading, that sums the whole thing up for you. That's where this one started – with the centurion's authority and his recognition of a similar quality in Jesus.

TELLING TIPS: Probably one to do on your own. Make sure you emphasize the first line in each section.

He was accustomed to having his way.

There were a hundred soldiers under his command, each one obliged to do whatever he wanted.

And as for the civilian population, there wasn't one of them who even dared to look him in the eye.

Fear? Hatred? It didn't matter – or so his fellow officers had often said. The point was to keep the peace. And if the odd busted head or broken arm or well-timed execution was the means it took to do that, so be it.

He was accustomed to having his way.

But in his experience, the stick was, on the whole, less effective than the carrot in that regard. And so, unlike some of his comrades, he took a more irenic approach to controlling the population of Palestine.

Yes, there were marches. Yes, there was a regular and visible military presence. But there were conversations, as well – particularly with the religious leaders. And the occasional contribution to some local cause.

Respect. That's what he was looking for. That's what he hoped he had achieved.

He was accustomed to having his way.

And then, one day, one of his servant boys fell ill. Deathly ill. And there was nothing he could do. No way to have his way. Not this time.

Somehow, word reached the synagogue. And the local religious officials paved the way for him to meet an itinerant teacher called Jesus.

The name was not strange to him. Protocol required keeping tabs on such men. They had a way of gathering crowds, then followers, then the kind of passionate momentum that had sometimes led to violence.

This man had the reputation for working miracles. And since a miracle was precisely what the centurion required, meeting the man seemed the thing to do.

He was accustomed to having his way.

That's the first thing the centurion thought when he saw Jesus.

The teacher did not look down. Not like the others. He looked the centurion in the eye, like they were equals. Maybe even like he was in charge.

On another occasion, the centurion thought, he might have taken this as a warning sign. But not now. Not when he needed what this man's reputation suggested he could provide.

And so it was the centurion who lowered his eyes.

"My servant is ill," he explained. "Paralyzed and in great pain. I understand that you have the power to heal him."

"I do," said Jesus. "And I will."

There was no doubt in the centurion's mind. The man said it. He would do it.

He was accustomed to having his way.

It wasn't a religious thing. It was more a matter of recognition. One man of power acknowledging the same trait in another.

And so, before Jesus could even take a step, the centurion held out his hand and said, "There's no need for you to come to the house. We are both men of authority. We know how this works. I tell my soldiers what to do, and they do it. The same is true of you. So say the word, and my servant will be healed."

And now it was the teacher's turn to be impressed.

"Did you hear that?" said Jesus to the crowd. "This man doesn't even share our faith, but there is not one of you who trusts me like he does. One day, I tell you, people just like him, from all over this world of ours, will come and feast with our forefathers in the kingdom of heaven!"

The centurion noted that the crowd did not seem to be particularly impressed by this. But their murmuring did not, for a moment, dampen the teacher's enthusiasm.

"Go," he said. "Your servant is already well."

The centurion had no doubt that he would find his servant healed. As for the teacher's confidence that people like him would find themselves in the company of his God, one day, the centurion was less sure.

But who knew?

The man was, after all, accustomed to having his way.

Questions

1. How do you think the crowd and Jesus' disciples felt when he agreed to help the centurion? Why might some in the crowd have questioned or resented this?

2. What do you think his followers and the others who were listening made of Jesus' remarks at the end?

3. Jesus lived among an oppressed people, and the centurion represented that oppression, even if he, personally, was kinder than most. Why didn't Jesus use this as an opportunity to address that oppression?

Only Five Miles

(Luke 7:11–17)

Introduction

Here's another reading that hinges on one idea. It's a guess, at best, but an interesting guess, nonetheless.

> **TELLING TIPS: Again, just read this one, with emphasis on the recurring line.**

She only lived five miles away.
  That's the distance from Nazareth to Nain.
  Granted, it probably seemed a lot further then than it does now.
  But still. Five miles. Just five miles.

So is it possible that when Jesus and his disciples stumbled across the funeral procession, he recognized her?
  Perhaps she was related to someone in Nazareth, and therefore a frequent visitor?
  Perhaps her husband, now deceased, had been a customer. One of Joseph's regular clients.
  Or perhaps it had been the other way round, and Joseph had bought from him. Tools, wood, other supplies. Who knows?
  It's just speculation. A guess.
  But five miles. Only five miles.

I suppose that in the face of that kind of grief – a widow losing her only son – Jesus would have been moved by the pain of a complete stranger. It happened in other times and at other places.
  But five miles. Just five miles.

And to walk up. To get so close. To touch the coffin. It's an act of familiarity. An act that might well have caused offence. But it went unchallenged. It was accepted. Was she so lost in her grief? Or did the woman know him?

Five miles. Only five miles.

And then the words. "Young man, get up!" To a corpse.

The mourners round Jairus's daughter would mock those words. But they were words from a complete stranger – a wonder-worker her father had just met in the street.

But what if these words were different? What if they were not just the widow's wishes? What if they were Jesus' wishes, as well – whispered out loud, and out of his grief, too.

What if he knew him? Remembered him as a boy? Racing round his father's shop? Alive.

I don't know. It's just a guess.

But Nazareth and Nain are just five miles apart.

Five miles. Only five miles.

Questions

1. Is it helpful, do you think, to ask questions of the text? To want to know or guess what else was going on?

2. What difference would it have made if the woman and her son were complete strangers? Does that make any difference to the story, seeing as we don't actually know one way or the other?

3. How would you have reacted if someone had walked up to a funeral you were a part of and ordered the deceased to get up?

Sowers and Soil and Seeds

(Luke 8:1–14)

Introduction

This one pretty much speaks for itself. It's a relatively straightforward retelling of Jesus' parable. It works really well in an all-age service.

TELLING TIPS: I have included the tips in the text, so they are easier to follow. Divide your group into four sections – that's probably the best way to do this. Then introduce the actions and practise them with each section before you start the story. Remember, the more fun you have with each action as you demonstrate it, the more likely it is that they will join in and enjoy it, too.

Jesus walked out of the house. He went to the lake – the lake of Galilee. But he didn't go to swim or to catch himself some fish. He went there to teach.

And when he sat down – 'cause that's what teachers did in those days – when he sat down, a huge crowd gathered round. So huge that they couldn't possibly see him, much less hear him.

So he borrowed a boat and pushed off a little way from shore. And when the people could see and when the people could hear, he told them a story, a particular kind of story we call a parable, a story with a special, hidden meaning.

"A farmer went out to sow some seed – tossing it here and there on the ground. Some of the seed fell on the hard, foot-worn path. And as soon as it did, the greedy birds swooped down and ate it up" *(gobble, gobble, gobble – hee-hee-hee – mmm)*.

"Some of the seed fell on rocks, where the soil was very shallow. The plants sprang up quickly" *(leap up to standing position – Ta-da! – or Hooray!)*. "But because the soil was shallow, their roots did not sink deep. And when the sun came up, it scorched them, and they withered and died" *("I'm melting! I'm melting" – à la* Wizard of Oz – *"Nooo!!" Drop into seat)*.

"Other seeds fell among the thorns" *(Uh-oh!)* "which grew up and choked the plants" *(put hands round own throat - GAAAH!)*.

"But some of the seed fell on good soil. And that produced a crop. A hundred, sixty, thirty times what was sown" *(cheer, "Fruit, fruit, that's what we're for. Thirty, sixty, a hundred times more! Goooo fruit!")*.

Jesus' disciples, his students, his apprentices, came to him and asked: "Why do you tell the people parables? Why not spell it out?"

"It gives them something to think about, to pray about, to puzzle over," said Jesus, "and if they have the ears to hear what God is saying, they'll get it. So here's what the parable means."

"The seed is the message of God's kingdom – all that I have come to teach you. When someone hears about it and does not understand it, he is like the seed on the path. The devil comes, like a greedy bird, and snatches it away" *(bird actions)*.

"The one who received the seed on the rocky place hears the message of the kingdom and accepts it with joy" *(stand up – Ta-da!)*. "But because he has no root, when trouble comes, he quickly withers away" *(wither motion)*.

"The next one accepts the message, too. And it sinks in and he grows. But then worry – worry about having too much stuff, worry about having too little, worry like a patch of thorns" *(Uh-oh!)* "comes along to choke him."

"And the last one is like the seed sown on good ground. He hears the message of the kingdom. He understands it. And his life is good and fruitful as a result" *(cheer, etc.)*.

Questions

1. One out of four seeds actually produces fruit. What do you think of that statistic? Is it realistic? Do you find it just a little depressing? Or is that reading too much into the story?

2. Which kind of ground do you think is most prevalent today? Among the people you know? And why?

3. Why do you think this is such a popular parable?

A Storm Story

(Luke 8:22–25)

Introduction

I have told this story a lot – but in one particular way, so it was difficult finding another way to tell it. I hope this works for you.

TELLING TIPS: See "Mary Meets an Angel" (above) for suggestions on how to tell this kind of story.

"Everybody in the boat!" Jesus said to his friends.
"Everybody in the boat!" Jesus said to his friends.
"Everybody in the boat!" Jesus said to his friends.
"It's time for us to cross the lake."
(Make shape of lake with fingers or wave motion.)
"It's time for us to cross the lake."
"It's time for us to cross the lake."

Jesus was tired, so he laid down his head,
Jesus was tired, so he laid down his head,
Jesus was tired, so he laid down his head,
And took a nap, a little power break.
(Lay head on hands, nap-like.)
And took a nap, a little power break.
And took a nap, a little power break.

As he was snoozing, a storm came down,
As he was snoozing, a storm came down,
As he was snoozing, a storm came down,

And that little boat began to shake.
(Shake.)
And that little boat began to shake.
And that little boat began to shake.

"Master, Master!" cried his friends. "We're going to drown!"
"Master, Master!" cried his friends. "We're going to drown!"
"Master, Master!" cried his friends. "We're going to drown!"
"Please stop sleeping, we need you awake!"
(Shake awake.)
"Please stop sleeping, we need you awake!"
"Please stop sleeping, we need you awake!"

So Jesus woke up – rebuked the wind and the rain:
So Jesus woke up – rebuked the wind and the rain:
So Jesus woke up – rebuked the wind and the rain:
"Stop your fussing, put on the brakes!"
(Pretend to put on brakes.)
"Stop your fussing, put on the brakes!"
"Stop your fussing, put on the brakes!"

The wind and the rain settled down at his command,
The wind and the rain settled down at his command,
The wind and the rain settled down at his command,
And his friends did a double-take.
(Do a double-take.)
And his friends did a double-take.
And his friends did a double-take.

"Where was your faith?" Jesus said to his friends.
"Where was your faith?" Jesus said to his friends.
"Where was your faith?" Jesus said to his friends.
"There was no need for you to quiver and quake."
(Quake – much like the shake.)
"There was no need for you to quiver and quake."
"There was no need for you to quiver and quake."

Then he laid his head back down and his friends began to whisper,
Then he laid his head back down and his friends began to whisper,
Then he laid his head back down and his friends began to whisper,
"He's someone special, there's no mistake!"
(Pretend to drop or spill something – oops!)
"He's someone special, there's no mistake!"
"He's someone special, there's no mistake!"

And they carried on across the lake.
(Lake motion again.)

Questions

1. Why do you think Luke included this miracle in his Gospel?

2. What's the point of it (other than rescuing the disciples, of course)?

3. Do you think the disciples were lacking in faith, or were they only acting like anyone would in their situation?

A Heart Story

(Luke 8:40–56)

Introduction

I find a lot of satisfaction in discovering a word or an image at the heart of a given story. And "heart" is most definitely the key word here!

> **TELLING TIPS: This is one to do on your own.**

His heart was breaking.

She was his only daughter.

She was only twelve.

And she was dying.

And in spite of his piety and his position in the community – ruler of the local synagogue – there was nothing that Jairus could do.

So he ran to Jesus and fell at his feet and begged, "Heal my daughter, please!"

Jesus agreed. And now Jairus's heart was racing. They were on their way, pushing through the crowded streets, when, suddenly, Jesus stopped.

"Who touched me?" he asked.

And even if time had not been an issue, Jairus thought, it would still have been a ridiculous question.

"There are people everywhere," one of his disciples observed. "Pressing on us all around."

"Point well made," nodded Jairus. But still Jesus dawdled.

"C'mon. C'mon. C'mon," he whispered, like a man in a traffic jam, late for an important date.

And then his heart sank.

"But I felt the power go out of me," Jesus announced, as if there was all the time in the world.

And then a woman spoke. "It was me," she said. "I'm the one who touched you."

And with a lorry on the left and a coach on the right and no place to turn and no exit in sight, all Jairus could do was stand there and wait, engine running, while the woman explained how twelve years of illness had suddenly come to an end.

"Twelve years, yes. Twelve years. That's all my daughter will have," was all he could think, "if this conversation doesn't finish soon."

But before it could, one of his servants appeared.

And Jairus's heart stopped.

That's what it felt like, anyway, because the look on the servant's face said it all.

"Your daughter is dead."

The servant said something else. "There's no need to bother the teacher, now." But it hardly registered. Jairus was alone. In a haze. Everything at a standstill.

And then somebody touched *him*.

"It will be all right," Jesus said. "Believe. And she will be healed."

So Jairus did. What else was left? What else could he do?

But as he approached the house, his heart began to ache. There was his family, wailing with the mourners. There was his wife, looking like there would be no tomorrow.

But Jesus acted as if nothing was the matter. He called three of his disciples to his side and strode right through the crowd.

"Stop your wailing," he said. "The girl's not dead. She's only sleeping."

And hopeful as that might have sounded, Jairus could not help feeling that it was a bit hard-hearted.

The crowd must have felt so, too – and they laughed at Jesus, in reply.

But he took no notice. Instead, he took the girl's hand, and like he was, indeed, waking her from a nap or a long night's rest, he simply said, "Get up, my child."

And she did.

And Jairus's heart? It leaped. It soared. It nearly broke again, but with joy this time.

And he pulled his child to his chest and held her there.

And just listened. Listened to her heart beat.

Questions

1. Put yourself in Jairus's place. Are the "heart" descriptions accurate? How would you have felt?

2. Given Jairus's anxiety and desperation, why do you think that Jesus was willing to stop and deal with the woman?

3. Have you ever been in a situation where, like Jairus, there was nothing you could do? What did God do in that situation?

A Bread Story

(Luke 9:10–17)

Introduction

Another one of those reasonably familiar stories where many in your group will probably know the outcome. That's one advantage of using a different kind of storytelling technique, because even if they know the story, once they hear the actions they'll be wondering how it all fits together!

> **TELLING TIPS: See "Mary Meets an Angel" (above) for suggestions on how to tell this kind of story.**

Jesus was teaching and healing one day,
Jesus was teaching and healing one day,
Jesus was teaching and healing one day,
When his friends came up to him and said:
(Hand to mouth and then move it forward.)
When his friends came up to him and said:
When his friends came up to him and said:

"We're far from the shops and these people are hungry.
"We're far from the shops and these people are hungry.
"We're far from the shops and these people are hungry.
Please send them somewhere to be fed."
(Eating/gobbling-up motion/sound.)
Please send them somewhere to be fed."
Please send them somewhere to be fed."

"Why don't you feed them?" Jesus said with a grin.
"Why don't you feed them?" Jesus said with a grin.
"Why don't you feed them?" Jesus said with a grin.

And all of his friends scratched their heads.
(Scratch head.)
And all of his friends scratched their heads.
And all of his friends scratched their heads.

"There are five thousand men – and their wives and their kids!
"There are five thousand men – and their wives and their kids!
"There are five thousand men – and their wives and their kids!
And we've got just two fish and some bread!"
(Pretend to break bread/loaf.)
And we've got just two fish and some bread!"
And we've got just two fish and some bread!"

"Why didn't I see that?" Jesus replied.
"Why didn't I see that?" Jesus replied.
"Why didn't I see that?" Jesus replied.
"I've obviously lost the thread.
(Sewing motion.)
"I've obviously lost the thread.
"I've obviously lost the thread.

Tell them all to sit down in groups of, say, fifty,
Tell them all to sit down in groups of, say, fifty,
Tell them all to sit down in groups of, say, fifty,
And we'll try something different, instead."
(Hand motion – as in "on the other hand".)
And we'll try something different, instead."
And we'll try something different, instead."

Then he prayed for the fish and he prayed for the bread,
Then he prayed for the fish and he prayed for the bread,
Then he prayed for the fish and he prayed for the bread,
His eyes shut, his arms outspread.
(Spread arms in praying pose.)
His eyes shut, his arms outspread.
His eyes shut, his arms outspread.

When he broke up the food, there was more than enough –
When he broke up the food, there was more than enough –
When he broke up the food, there was more than enough –
Enough to fill up a shed!
(Trace shape of shed with fingers.)
Enough to fill up a shed!
Enough to fill up a shed!

And everyone ate and no one went hungry –
And everyone ate and no one went hungry –
And everyone ate and no one went hungry –
Every Tom, Dick, and Harry,
And Carol and Betty,
And Barney and Wilma,
And Fred.
(Shout "Yabba-dabba-do!")
Every Tom, Dick, and Harry,
And Carol and Betty,
And Barney and Wilma,
And Fred.
Every Tom, Dick, and Harry,
And Carol and Betty,
And Barney and Wilma,
And Fred.

Questions

1. This story is so familiar that it sometimes loses its "bite". How do you react if you're in the crowd? What's your first thought? And what do you think when someone tells you what actually happened?

2. Some biblical commentators suggest that Jesus simply set an example for the crowd through the boy's generosity. And then they pulled out their packed lunches and shared – and that was the "real miracle". What problems do you see with this interpretation, given the way the story is told and also given what happened afterwards (see the next story).

3. What do you suppose is the "point" of this miracle?

Popping Down to Tesco's

(John 6)

Introduction

I wrote this little piece in response to a "situation" I discovered at one of the churches I pastored. We used lots of different speakers on a Sunday morning, and it turned out that some folks were deciding to come (or not) depending on who was speaking. Some of them had even organized a phone chain. Yikes!

So I made it clear that church is not like Tesco's or Asda or the local restaurant, where we move around if we don't like what's on the menu. Some folks had a hard time grasping this. They reckoned that, like everything else in their lives, church was all about choice – and they were the consumers! Now we're members of a community, not consumers, I countered – who need each other and depend upon each other and who are called to minister to each other, regardless of who is speaking at the front.

I suppose, in a way, that we have only ourselves to blame for all of this. And by that, I mean we clergy types. That's why I stuck the church growth guy in the reading. Yeah, I understand the benefits of the whole church growth thing: demographics, targets, location, etc. But the fact that all that same kind of effort goes into building a new shopping centre or plunking down a new fast-food restaurant in a community only adds to the confusion, I think, and the misconception that church members are nothing more than customers who can (and perhaps even ought to) move on to the next restaurant when the current one no longer meets their needs – with little thought given to the needs that might be met by their continued commitment to that less-than-perfect community. Thus endeth the sermon. Here's the reading.

TELLING TIPS: One to do on your own (that's just about how Jesus ended up).

So Jesus fed five thousand men. And their wives. And their children.

And when the left-overs had all been gathered and tucked away in Tupperware, the crowd decided that he would make a more-than-adequate Messiah, and sought to place a crown upon his head.

Jesus wanted no part of this, and seeking to escape, found a short-cut across the middle of a stormy lake. And when the people, who were forced to take the long way round the shore, finally caught up with him, they were, understandably, hungry once again. So, mouths drooling, and tummies grumbling, they looked to him for another slap-up meal.

And that's when Jesus turned to them and said (in as many words), "You're not looking for God, at all, are you? You're looking for Tesco's."

The crowd hemmed and hawed a bit, shuffling their sandals, looking down at their feet. But in the end, they had to admit that he was right.

"God fed our ancestors in the desert," they shrugged. "And, well, we sort of thought that you might do the same. So, yeah, Tesco's. Or Asda. Or even Aldi's will do. Just so's we get a bit more grub."

"I've got something even better to give you," Jesus explained. And while their minds raced to visions of a three-courser at the newest Jamie Oliver, he told them he was the bread of life, and that if they ate of him they would never go hungry again.

Frankly, they had trouble getting their heads round that, not to mention their bicuspids. They hadn't walked all the way around a lake for symbolic nosh, nor for allegorical comestibles. They wanted their bellies filled. And when Jesus explained that that simply was not going to happen, there ensued a scene not unlike that moment in *Back to the Future* when Marty McFly plays the extended guitar solo at the sock hop. The crowd stared at him, silent, wide-eyed, jaws dropped to the floor, a cricket chirrupping in the distance. Or quite possibly not a cricket, but a church growth expert scribbling something on a bit of paper about how not to create a seeker-sensitive congregation.

And then they left. One by one. Ten by ten. Hundreds by hundreds. Grumbling. Hungry. Disappointed. Off to look for another church – one that met their needs.

And Jesus turned to The Twelve. His apprentices. His disciples. His mates.

"Are you off, too?" he asked.

And Peter answered for the rest: "Not likely! Where else will we find the word of life?"

And Jesus smiled. And the church growth expert scratched his head. Five thousand down to twelve in a day. He wouldn't be asking Jesus to lead any workshops come the next convention.

The difference?

Jesus wasn't looking for five thousand people who wanted the All You Can Eat Buffet.

He was looking for twelve who wanted to change the world.

Now there's something to chew on.

Questions

1. So do you think I'm being a bit harsh here? Is there ever a good reason for leaving a church?

2. What do you think? I see a lot more church-hopping as people feel more and more like consumers. Is there an answer to this?

3. How does any given church define "success"? How do you define it? What about Jesus?

And Jesus Was Confused

(John 7:53–8:11)

Introduction

All right, then – it looks like the tricky readings have all come together. Much like the last piece, this one arose from a contemporary pastoral situation.

There have been several books written lately, complaining that the public perception of the church, particularly among the young, is that it is too judgmental – specifically where sexual matters are concerned (and more specifically with regard to the gay community). Much better to just follow Jesus, these books suggest, than to get oneself wrapped up in tradition-bound, judgmental institutions – as if Jesus was some kind of fluffy bunny who never judged anyone.

Now I know that the passage upon which the following reading is based does not appear in every ancient manuscript. But it is a reasonably familiar story, and it's not the only one where Jesus is actually critical of someone else's lifestyle (you will find a similar piece to this one when you get round to the Rich Young Ruler). I just thought it would be interesting and informative and ironic to toss some of the arguments that currently get tossed at the church in Jesus' direction and to see how absurd they really are.

> **TELLING TIPS: You need to read aloud the story of the Woman Caught in Adultery (John 7:53–8:11) and then follow it with the reading below.**

And the woman turned to Jesus and said, "I'm sorry. What did you say?"

Jesus smiled and said it again: "Go. And leave your life of sin."

"That's what I thought you said," the woman responded. But she did not smile back. "So you think I'm a sinner, do you? Leading a life of sin, as you call it? Typical! Religious people! I should have expected this."

Jesus looked confused.

"All right, you don't have a stone in your hand," she continued. "Thanks very much. But your attitude is just the same as the ones who did. Condemnation, just because I'm different to you!"

Jesus tried to answer, but the woman was speaking more quickly now and hardly taking a breath.

"Who are you...?" – her face was growing red – "who are you to judge the manner in which I express my sexuality? I like sex. I like lots of it. It makes me happy. It's the way I'm made. Why can't you just accept that and keep your opinions to yourself?"

Again, Jesus tried to answer her, but it was no use.

"Did it ever occur to you that everybody is different? That we don't all fit into your cosy little understanding of the place and purpose of sex?

"Oh, I know what you're going to say. 'The Law says...' The Law says! I've heard it a hundred times before from teachers just like you. Well, let me tell you this, Mr Rabbi. The Law was written hundreds of years ago by men *(men!)* from a different time and a different place and it doesn't begin to address the needs of people living in this century!

"So spare me your judgment and your condescension. I love my life, just the way it is. And as it happens, I love the man I was sleeping with. So there! And if it's somehow wrong to express that love in a way that makes us both feel good – well, then, there's something wrong with this world. That's all I can say.

"And as for sin – has it never occurred to you that intolerance is a sin, as well? Maybe the biggest sin of them all? And if that's the case, mister, I'm not the one who needs to 'leave my life of sin' – you are!"

And with that, she turned and left.

And Jesus? He shook his head. He'd saved the woman, quite literally – and offered her the chance to be saved in every other way. So he stooped down and began to scratch in the dirt again. And what he scratched was a great big "?"

Questions

1. Too harsh? Missed the point? Or spot on? Discuss.

2. The church is, as I have suggested, often criticized for being too judgmental, particularly where sex is concerned. My impression, though, is that the church has largely backed away from this (perhaps so as not to seem out of touch with the times – or too much like our parents!). The problem, as I see it, is that the old false god, Sex, is still pretty much at work in this world, maybe even more so, claiming all sorts of victims through addiction to pornography, and STDs, and broken families, and abortions, and – well, I could go on. Do you think the church has made a mistake in retreating from these areas? And how can we be truly prophetic in these areas again?

3. Do you think the church is more judgmental than Jesus? In what ways?

Saints and Screw-ups: a Joke for Sometime in the Future

(Luke 9:18–27; Matthew 16)

Introduction

One minute you're doing the thing God called you to – doing it well – doing what's right. And then, next minute – sometimes literally the next minute – you're messing up again. That's Peter's story in a nutshell, particularly in Matthew chapter 16. And it is so often my story, too.

Since most people don't know my mess-ups, however, I thought it might be interesting and helpful and ultimately gracious to contrast Peter's contradictory responses to Jesus with a more contemporary example of the same sort of thing.

> **TELLING TIPS:** You'll need two readers for this one. Oh, and a voice-over. An American Deep Southern accent will work best for Jim Bakker. Not so sure about Peter. In the book of Acts, he gets criticized for having an uneducated Galilean accent. You could try that.

Voice-over: So did you hear the one about St Peter and Jim Bakker at the Pearly Gates?

Peter: I was a disciple.

Jim: I was an evangelist.

Peter: We were in the region of Caesarea Philippi.

Jim: I was in the beautiful city of Charlotte, North Carolina.

Peter: Jesus asked us, "Who do folks say that I am?"

Jim: Jesus told me, "Go and preach the word."

Peter: Someone said, "John the Baptist."

Jim:	I was Pentecostal, but denominations didn't mean a thing to me.
Peter:	Someone said, "Elijah."
Jim:	Those were the days! God's fiery judgment raining down as I spoke.
Peter:	Some said, "Jeremiah."
Jim:	I was a young man, yes, but the Lord moved powerfully.
Peter:	And some said, "One of the other prophets." *Hab*akkuk, as I recall. Or maybe I just like the way it sounds.
Jim:	We say "Ha*bakk*uk", but I still love you, brother.
Peter:	And then it happened – my *big* moment.
Jim:	Television! That's what they told me. You need to be on television, boy!
Peter:	God gave me the words.
Jim:	Indeed he did – and we broadcast them coast to coast!
Peter:	"You are Jesus, the Messiah, the Son of the Living God!"
Jim:	And they came to him, in their thousands and their tens of thousands! Yeah, I know what they say – hands on the TV, the wife's mascara running. Sure, there was a show. But folks got saved, folks got changed.
Peter:	"This is not from you. This is from God," he said.
Jim:	It was. It totally was. I could never have done that on my own.
Peter:	"On this rock, I will build my church," he said.
Jim:	And boy, did we build one! And a theme park, too. Bigger than a hundred football fields.
Peter:	"You get to bind. You get to loose," he said. "And here are the keys. The Keys to the Kingdom."
Jim:	The keys to the mansion. The keys to the Porsche. The keys to the safety deposit box. The keys were the start of the downfall. The beginning of the end.
Peter:	And maybe that was true for me, as well. The keys. I thought I had a lock on the truth – that I had it all figured out.
Jim:	All. Figured. Out. Don't I know it!
Peter:	He said we were going to Jerusalem. He told us he was going to die, that sacrifice was at the heart of what he came to do.

Jim:	Sacrifice? I'd left sacrifice way behind. Now it was all about reaping the rewards.
Peter:	"Sacrifice?" I laughed. "Surely you don't mean that? Not for the Messiah? Not for the Son of God?"
Jim:	And not for his spokesman either. Not when there were fortunes to be made and women to be laid.
Peter:	And that's when he turned to me...
Jim:	And that's when they turned on me...
Together:	*(looking at each other?)* ... and said, "Get behind me, Satan."
Peter:	And I was shocked.
Jim:	And I was divorced.
Peter:	And I was devastated.
Jim:	And I was bankrupted.
Peter:	And I was impaled through the heart by the look on his face.
Jim:	And I was imprisoned and served my time.
Peter:	And I was never the same again.
Jim:	And I was never the same either.
Peter:	But I got things right in the end.
Jim:	And so did I, I believe.
Peter:	By his grace.
Jim:	Yeah, only by his grace.
Peter:	And that's why he put me here.
Jim:	At the Pearly Gates?
Peter:	To tell my story and remind everyone who arrives that we're all heroes and goats.
Jim:	All saints and screw-ups.
Peter:	And to unlock the gates with the key.
Jim:	Which is...?
Peter:	His grace. *(He unlocks, they look up.)*
Jim:	Only his grace. *(Pause.)* You know, they don't look all that "pearly", actually.
Peter:	Everybody says that. I've always thought they were more of an off-white.
Jim:	Cream, I'd say.
Peter:	Or maybe Olde English White. Like one of those classic Jags.
Jim:	Nice. I had one of those. Once.
Peter:	So, are you ready to come in?

Jim:	You bet! A televangelist walking through the Pearly Gates. Some people would think that's the perfect joke.
Peter:	The joke's on all of us, my friend. And the best thing of all? We get to laugh about it. Forever…

Questions

1. Think about a time when you were a saint and a screw-up. How did that work out?

2. Are there any other contemporary examples I might have used?

3. So if God's gonna forgive, does it matter that we screw up? Why or why not?

Glow, Moses, Glow!

(Luke 9:28–36)

Introduction

First of all, apologies to Graham Kendrick. He's a nice guy with a good sense of humour, so I'm hoping he will understand that when I was asked to write a song about the Transfiguration, there was really no other choice. "Shine, Jesus, Shine!" That's what it's all about. So "Shine, Jesus, Shine!" had to be at the heart of it. Yes, I nicked the odd lyric just for familiarity's sake. And, yes, seeing as Elijah is knocking about in the story, I had to nick the odd line from Robin Mark as well (again, apologies). But people really like this song. It's loads of fun. So enjoy!

> **TELLING TIPS: Sing it to the tune of "Shine, Jesus, Shine". Simple as that. And even though it's a parody, you mustn't forget to mark it down on your music licence sheet. Graham deserves something for all this abuse, after all!**

Jesus said to Peter, "Let's go up the mountain."
Took so many steps that he could hardly count 'em.
James and John came along for the journey.
Suddenly Jesus started to transform, he
Shone like the sun,
Shone like the sun.

Shine, Jesus, Shine,
Fill this land with the Father's glory,
Glow, Moses, Glow,
Look! He's stood there, as well!
These are the days, are the days,

Hey look, there's the prophet Elijah!
He's shining, too
And we're all feeling swell!

Peter said to Jesus, "Why not build three tents near?
One for you and these other two gents here?"
Then God came down in a big shiny cloud.
"This is my Son," he said. "He's made me proud.
Listen to him
(I want you to) Listen to him!"

Chorus

When the cloud had lifted Jesus stood there alone.
They went back down the mountain, Peter walked on his own.
"Oh dear," he thought, "I've gone and put my foot in it."
But then he reconsidered. "Hey, wait just a minute!
I know what Jesus means.
I said it back in chapter 16!"

Chorus

Questions

1. All kidding aside, why do you suppose Jesus let his disciples see the Transfiguration?

2. Why do you suppose that Peter wanted to build the tents/booths?

3. And why did Moses and Elijah join Jesus? Why not Abraham and – I don't know – Habakkuk?

The Great Grand-lamma-lamma

(Luke 9:46–50)

Introduction

OK, this one gets a little silly. But it was late. I was on a roll. I needed something to make me chuckle. Hope you chuckle, too.

TELLING TIPS: You could do this on your own, quite easily. Or you could get twelve helpers to practise it and do it with you, each of them doing one of the disciple lines. Or you could pick twelve volunteers at random (make sure you know them reasonably well), stick the lines up on a screen (one at a time, to maintain the surprise – one slide for each line, that sort of thing) and have them read them as you point to them in turn. The chaos of seeing and then having to say each line at that precise moment could add to the fun. And it could just as easily be disastrous!

So the disciples started to argue – about which of them would be the greatest. Which is not unusual, I suppose, seeing as they were training to be rabbis and there were, presumably, good rabbis and lousy rabbis and downright brilliant rabbis whose reputation lasted for generations.

Paul, you will recall, boasted on more than one occasion that he was trained at the feet of the Rabbi Gamaliel – who was, apparently, no slouch. Paul was also the only apostle who missed this little lesson. If that doesn't explain the tone of some of his letters, nothing will.

Anyway, the disciples were arguing.

One of them said, "I'll be the greatest."

And another answered, "Ridiculous! I'll be greater than you!"

To which a third replied, "I'll be the great-granddaddy greatest of you all!"

And so another suggested, "I'll be the great-granddaddy's grand-lamma-lamma."

To which another said, "Well, I'll be the guru of the great-granddaddy's grand-lamma-lamma."

And another said, "I'll be the mother of the guru of the great-granddaddy's grand-lamma-lamma."

And another replied, "Grandmother of the guru of the great-granddaddy's grand-lamma-lamma."

In response to which another said, "Infinity" (well, someone had to break that lamma thing).

To which another said, "Googleplex."

To which another said, "Google."

To which another said, "Yahoo."

To which another said, "Jeeves."

To which they all said, "Jeeves? Are you out of your mind? You can never find anything on Jeeves!"

To which Jesus said, "Listen up, boys, I've got something to say." And he stood a little child beside him and said, "Whoever stoops down to welcome this little child, welcomes me. And whoever welcomes me, welcomes the one who sent me. For the one who is least among you is the one who is greatest of all."

Then Jesus took the child back to his parents. And when he had gone, the disciples looked at one another, shrugged their shoulders, and muttered, "Great."

Questions

1. Do you think my explanation as to why they might have been discussing the "greatest" thing is valid? What other explanation might there be?

2. So what was Jesus getting at when he used the example of welcoming the child? It's not like other places, where he says they need to be like the child. And where did he get the child? Just like that, I mean. Did he leave them to their argument, wander off, find a friendly family, ask to borrow their kid, explain the reason, and then return? I guess there might have been time – particularly if the Aramaic for "great-grand-lamma-lamma" makes it even longer to say.

3. Anyway – what's "great" in Jesus' book?

Foxes, Funerals and Furrows

(Luke 9:57–62)

Introduction

A little reading, this one, but I think it sums up nicely the intent of these three sayings.

"Foxes have holes," said Jesus. "Birds have nests. But I have nowhere to lay my head. No furniture, no flat, no financial security. Know that first, if you would follow me."

"Funerals are for dead men," said Jesus. "Even a funeral as important as your father's. But the Kingdom of God is more important still. Put that first, if you would follow me."

"Furrows in a field need to be straight and true," said Jesus. "And facing forward is the only way to plough them. You'll never do it looking back. The future comes first, if you would follow me."

Foxes, Funerals, and Furrows.
Come and follow me.

Questions

1. Do you think that Jesus makes following him sound even more difficult than it really is? Or less?

2. Can you think of any specific examples in your own experience of following Jesus that correspond to the pictures he paints here? Discuss.

3. Is Jesus exaggerating for effect, or does he really mean it?

Not a Story about Loving

(Luke 10:25–37)

Introduction

I love it when I find something in a really familiar story that I never noticed before. That's what occasioned this retelling of the story of the Good Samaritan. I hope at least some of you will be surprised as well!

> **TELLING TIPS: You could do this as a two-hander, with one of you reading the main text (telling the story) and the other doing the two-line chorus-y bit.**

A man asks Jesus a question.
   "How do I inherit eternal life?"
   So Jesus gives him an answer.
   "Love God with all you've got. And love your neighbour as yourself."
   This sounds hard, and a bit extreme. Like a room without walls. A country without borders. "Surely there are limits," thinks the man.
   So he asks a follow-up question.
   "Who, exactly, is my neighbour?"
   And Jesus tells him a story.
   But it's not a story about loving.
   It's not about loving, at all.

A man walks down a dangerous road. From Jerusalem to Jericho. And he has a nasty surprise.
   He is set upon by thieves. Robbed and left for dead. Hopeless.
   It's not a story about loving.
   It's not about loving, at all.

So two men come along, a priest and a Levite. It's starting to sound like a joke. But they don't walk into a bar. And the wounded man is definitely not laughing.

And instead of helping him, they pass by, presumably because they are both temple officials and they don't want to make themselves unclean. And touching blood (of which there is plenty) or touching a dead body (of which there is quite possibly one – they don't get close enough to check!) would do just that. And so, in order to keep one of God's laws, they violate another. And they leave the man alone.

This is, of course, one of the official explanations for their behaviour. The only problem I have with it is that they are walking away from Jerusalem, which means they have already done their jobs, which means that helping the man wouldn't have kept them from performing their temple functions, which means they could have touched him, which means, at the end of the day, that maybe, just maybe, they didn't actually give a monkey's!

So it's still not a story about loving.

It's not about loving, at all.

And then another man comes by. A Samaritan man. A man whom the wounded man would quite likely have considered a heretic and a half-breed, well outside of God's love and grace. In fact, it's quite possible that the wounded man was on that road in the first place because it was the best road for avoiding the territory of the Samaritan man. Ironic, yeah?

But the Samaritan man helps the wounded man. He dresses his wounds, and bundles him onto his beast, and takes him to the nearest emergency room, and pays for both his treatment and the rehab that follows.

And it's still not a story about loving.

It's not about loving, at all.

Because if it was about loving, then surely the roles would have been reversed. The Samaritan would have been the wounded man. And the man on the donkey would have been – I don't know – the man who asked the question. The man who wanted to know how far love should go.

But Jesus knew his heart. And he knows ours too. He knew that if the Samaritan had been the victim, and the other man the helper, then his message might still have been missed.

Help a hated enemy? Stoop to give aid to a foe? It looks like love, sure. But it might just be condescension or pity – another way of looking down on someone, even as you're reaching down to pull them up.

But when you are the one who is in trouble, who is left for dead, who is left without hope unless someone helps, then "loving your neighbour" is all that matters. Or rather, receiving love from him. And that's the point of the story. And it's genius.

Because it's not a story about loving, at all.

It's a story about being loved.

Questions

1. So what do you think of this approach to the story? Agree or disagree? And does it make any difference?

2. Think of a time when you found yourself in a similar situation – no, I don't mean beaten up and left for dead at the side of some road in Palestine (though, if that does apply, it would be interesting). I mean a time when you had to be rescued, helped by someone you didn't particularly like.

3. What is the essence of love, then – as revealed in this story?

They Were Sisters

(Luke 10:38–41)

Introduction

A short story, this – but lots going on. It happens quickly. Boom-boom. So the telling has to reflect that.

TELLING TIPS: Two readers (1 is Martha, 2 is Mary), who need to read their parts as if they were those characters, particularly when they do the same line together. And watch carefully near the end, when the order gets mixed up a bit.

1: She was busy.
2: She was calm.
1: She was frustrated.
2: She was intrigued.
1 & 2: She was overwhelmed.

1: She knew her place.
2: She knew what she wanted.
1: She was distracted.
2: She was focused.
1 & 2: It was all she could do to keep from bursting.

1: Lord, she's left me with all the work. Don't you care?
2: She was embarrassed.
1: She was fed up to the teeth.
1& 2: So Jesus spoke.

1:    You're worried and upset, Martha, that's clear. But there's only one thing that's necessary here.

2:    Mary has chosen that – chosen what is better. And that will not be taken away from her.

1:    Was she satisfied?

2:    Was she justified?

1:    Did she listen, as well?

2:    Did she get up and help?

1:    We don't know.

2:    Don't even know why.

1 & 2:   *(looking at each other)* Maybe nobody dared to say.

Questions

1. So what do you think happened in the end?

2. Are you a Mary or a Martha?

3. Do you think Martha's frustration was in any way justified? Was Mary doing more than just annoying her sister? Was she out of place? And is Jesus saying something here about the relative merits of housework and Bible study? Or is this more complex?

Little Light Shine

(Luke 11:33–36)

Introduction

Another little song. Again you could make up your own tune, or listen to a clip of the tune that I use on my website (www.kregel.com/bobhartman). I'm not sure it covers any territory missed by "This Little Light of Mine". But it's newer and you do get to go *"Ow!"*

> **TELLING TIPS: Teach the actions as you teach/sing each line. I have put them in the text for convenience's sake. As ever, the more you enjoy the actions when you teach them, the more likely your group will be to "play along".**

If you let your little light shine (hands like lights flashing)
Men will see your deeds are fine (thumbs up)
And they'll say, "Your God's divine!" (point finger in air)
If you let your little light shine (as in line 1).

1. You are a city,
   Set on a mountain high.
   Everyone will stop and stare
   As they go passing by.

Chorus

2. You are a lamp,
   Burning bright upon a stand.
   Don't cover it up with a bowl or a cup
   And definitely not with your hand.
   (Remove hand quickly and shout "Ow!")

Chorus

Questions

1. How exactly do we let our lights shine?

2. How do we do that without being seen as show-offs or identified as holier-than-thou?

3. Discuss contemporary examples where you saw someone's light shine in a way that accomplished what this song/scripture suggests is possible.

A Modern Parable of the Rich Fool

(Luke 12:16–21)

(With apologies to the translators of the Authorized Version and none whatsoever to Bernie Madoff)

Introduction

Yeah, this reading is going to date. Eventually, folks will forget who Bernie Madoff is, but I bet it takes a while. And I also figure that there will always be some other well-known greedy so-and-so to fill his shoes. So substitute if you need to, down the line.

TELLING TIPS: This is one for you to read on your own. You might want to mention that it's dedicated to Mr Madoff, or read the parenthetical bit after the title.

The investments of a certain rich man brought forth plentifully.

And he thought within himself, saying, "What shall I do, because I have no way with which to increase my cash flow?"

And he said, "This will I do. I will pull down the sound economic mechanisms I have heretofore employed. And, on the basis of my reputation, I will build something greater. I will invite my friends, and their friends, and their friends' friends to join me in a shady financial scheme.

"And my friends will bestow their fruits on me. And their friends will bestow their fruits on them. And their friends' friends will bestow their fruits on their friends. And it will last forever. Like the pyramids.

"And I will say to my soul, 'Soul, thou hast much goods laid up for many years. Take thine ease, eat, drink, and be merry.'"

But the Judge said unto him, "Thou fool! This night thy life shall be required of thee (or a portion thereof, amounting to not less than 150 years). Then whose shall those things be, which thou hast laid up?"

So is he that layeth up treasure for himself, and is not rich towards God.

Questions

1. Why do you think that Jesus is so hard on rich guys?

2. Maybe you are rich (actually, if you live in the "West" you fit in that category – at least as far as the rest of the world is concerned). How do readings like this make you feel?

3. Is there anything good about having riches – as far as the New Testament goes?

Thinkin' 'bout Ravens

(Luke 12:22–34)

Introduction

I got into this little "thinkin' 'bout" groove, and the following three readings were the result.

> **TELLING TIPS: It might help to read this passage from Scripture first, before you do the reading. It will familiarize your group with the passage and I think they will enjoy this "riff" on it a whole lot more.**

Think about ravens for a minute.
   Oversized crows. Edgar Alan Poe. Got it?
   Now answer me this:
   Have you ever seen a raven ploughing a field?
   Thought not.
   Or driving a combine harvester?
   Nope.
   Forking hay into a barn? Filling a silo?
   Not even "nevermore". Just plain "never".
   Yet God feeds them all they need.

Now think about lilies.
   Tall white Easter lilies. Stripey orange tiger lilies. Pad-perching water lilies. Got it?
   Now answer me this:
   Have you ever seen a lily looking for work?
   "Gizza job."
   Thought not.

Or doing that Rapunzel thing with a spinning-wheel?

Nope.

Or picking through the racks at the local Topshop?

And, speaking of fashion, lilies last just about as long as the latest style.

Yet God makes them beautiful.

So don't worry. God will do the same for you.

And now I know what you're thinking. I don't even have to ask.

That's crazy. That's barmy. That's nuts!

And so I'll ask again.

Think about ravens.

Think about lilies.

Are they crazy?

Nope (unless you want to count pecking out the innards of roadkill).

They do what God made them to do and let him take care of the rest.

And that's all he asks of us.

To do what he made us for.

Love him.

Love one another.

Look for his kingdom.

And leave him to take care of the rest.

Consider the ravens.

Consider the lilies.

Questions

1. Is Jesus' advice here in any way practical? How?

2. Is this hyperbole, or does he really mean it?

3. What specific difference would it make to your life if you took this seriously?

Thinkin' 'bout Mustard

(Luke 13:18–21)

Introduction

This one's a little longer – a bit of a sermon, really ('cause that's how it started). It gets there in the end, though – and there's plenty of food for thought. Well, plenty of mustard and bread, anyway.

TELLING TIPS: Don't forget to do the 1 Corinthians reading near the end. It won't make much sense otherwise.

Think about mustard for a minute.

That's right. Mustard.

English. French. The bright yellow hot-doggy stuff. Whatever.

Jesus said that the kingdom of God is like a mustard seed. Maybe the smallest seed of all. But a seed that grows into an enormous tree, where birds build their homes in the branches.

So you need to know something about mustard.

And you need to know something about bread. Well, yeasty bread – no pittas permitted.

So think about bread.

White. Wheat. Whatever. Roll-shaped. Baguette-ish. Loaf-like.

It's yeast that makes it rise. Leaven is what Jesus called it. And he said that the kingdom of God is like leaven. And when just a little of it gets mixed into the dough, it makes enough to feed a crowd.

So you need to know something about bread.

And finally, I suppose, you need to know something about the kingdom of God. Now I could go on and on. Plenty of theologians have. But this is supposed to be a reading, not a lecture, so let's borrow Jesus' definition. You can find it in the prayer he taught us.

"Thy kingdom come"? It's when God's will is done – on earth as it is in heaven.

So, given a little space – a mustard-seed-sized door, a leaven's worth – surrendering to the will of God can result in some very big changes – to you and me, to our communities, to our churches, to the world.

And there you have it. Except of course, you don't. Because that surrender thing doesn't come easy. Not to any of us.

And what is more, mustard seeds don't grow into trees. Not big ones with bird-burdened branches. No, mustard seeds grow into shrubs. And not very pretty shrubs, as it happens. Quite weedy shrubs, in fact, that people used to yank out of their gardens.

So what's up? Did Jesus get it wrong? Does divine knowledge not extend to horticulture?

I can't answer that one. But I can say that there is just the chance that Jesus had a different tree in mind, altogether.

You see, there's this vision in the book of Daniel. One of King Nebuchadnezzar's vision. And the vision – are you still with me? – is of a tree! A great big tree. A great big tree with birds in its branches. A-ha!

And what does Daniel say that the great big tree stands for? A great big kingdom!

So maybe what Jesus is really saying to his listeners is this: the tiny little mustard seed, which you think is just a weed, will grow into the biggest kingdom you ever heard of!

And then, to add insult to injury, he brings up yeast. Yeah, yeast. I've got no problem with yeast. You've got no problem. But to his listeners, yeast was the thing that made bread bad. Because all sacred bread was yeast-less. Un-leavened. Pure.

So maybe what Jesus is really saying is this: God's kingdom is like yeast – the thing you think is impure will be the thing that works its way into the dough and feeds a multitude.

Weeds and seeds and impure stuff – that's what's at the heart of God's kingdom. That's what makes the difference. That's what leads to the surrender. That's what makes the kingdom come.

And how is that? I think Paul had it all figured out. *(Read 1 Corinthians 1:20–25.)*

The Mustard seed. The weed.
The leaven – no taste of heaven.
The cross. The loss. The curse.
From such the kingdom comes.

You just need to know something about mustard.
And you need to know something about bread.

Questions

1. So what do you think of this way of looking at the passage? OK? Rubbish? Huh?

2. Can you think of any other examples where understanding a bit more about what things were like in the first century makes the passage clearer?

3. What kind of comfort, if any, do you find in the idea that God uses rubbishy stuff to fix the world?

Thinkin' 'bout Foxes and Chickens

(Luke 13:31–35)

Introduction

One more to think about. It's an interesting contrast, don't you think?

> **TELLING TIPS: One to do on your own. Or you might want to have someone help you. A reader for each critter.**

Think about foxes for a minute.
    That's right. Foxes.
    Sly as a fox.
    Crazy like a fox.
    Cute little heartbreaker. Sweet little lovemaker.
    Foxy Lady.
    Sleek. Sexy. Self-sufficient.
    Foxes.

Think about foxes. Now think again.
    'Cause Jesus called King Herod a fox.
    And, by implication, all those religious leaders in Israel's sad and long history who relied on their instinct and their cunning and their wiles to save their nation. And who put the prophets to death for simply suggesting that trusting God and doing his will and turning back to him might be a more effective course.
    So the prophets died. And, ironically, the leaders did too. For sleek and sexy and self-sufficient so often leads to slavery.

Now think about chickens.

That's right. Chickens.

"Don't be a chicken!" your friends jeer, when you're the only one who hasn't jumped off the diving-board.

"Don't be a chicken!" your dad chides, when your knuckles are white on the side of the slide.

Nobody wants to be a chicken.

Cowardly.

Cringeing.

Kentucky-fried.

Think about chickens. Now think again.

'Cause that's what Jesus hoped and prayed those prophet-killing foxes might become. Chickens. Chicks. Running towards him like he was their mother hen. Wings outstretched. To protect. To comfort. To save.

So we can be foxes. Sleek and self-sufficient. Making our own way. Cleverly paving a path to destruction.

Or we can be chickens. Running to him. Running his way. Safe under his arms. Outstretched.

Don't be a chicken?

Don't be an idiot.

Don't be a fox.

Questions

1. Another case (like the rich man) where Jesus warns us not to rely on our own resources, but to trust God instead. Doesn't that just make us dependent? Wouldn't it be better to be self-sufficient? Discuss.

2. Find out something about Herod. Was he really a "fox"? In what ways? Clue – he's not the one in the Christmas story. You might want to check under "John the Baptist, head, platter", instead.

3. Why would anybody want to be a chicken?

Hospitality

(Luke 14:1–23)

Introduction

A bit of a mouthful, this one. And it covers a lot of territory. But the overall direction is pretty clear and it does (to paraphrase The Dude) "tie the passage together".

> **TELLING TIPS: You could break this one up by having someone else read the Bible passages in chunks and then using the reading in between. I'll let you do the breaking into chunks bit. You know what your needs are. So show some initiative. Or (to paraphrase the other Lebowski) "Don't be a bum, sir!"**

So Jesus gets invited to a dinner party. He gets the chance to sample some of that famous Middle Eastern hospitality. But as luck would have it, it's a Pharisee who is hosting this little soirée. And hospitality is the last thing on his mind.

"He was being carefully watched." That's what the Bible says. They were keeping their eyes on Jesus.

Like paparazzi following a movie star.

Like the gutter press hanging onto a candidate's every syllable.

Just waiting for that embarrassing photo, that awkward sentence, that misstep, that mistake, that gaffe.

So Jesus obliges them.

There's a guest at the table with dropsy. Which is an old word for oedema. Which is a medical term for swelling. Which is often, though not always, due to congestive heart failure. So you can imagine the guest's surprise/delight/relief when Jesus reaches over and heals him.

"Everyone all right with that?" Jesus asks, knowing full well that it's the

Sabbath. And that it's against the law to work on the Sabbath. And that healing congestive heart failure is most definitely work. You can ask your GP.

The hospitable thing would have been to respond. But hospitality, remember, is in short supply around this table. So they just stare at him – like a left-wing politician who has just finished reading the latest Clarkson piece.

Offended by the blatant political incorrectness of the thing. Can't believe the cheek. But it's good. (Note to aide: Jag XF. Clarkson rates it. Probably room for it in the expense account.)

And then (a bit like Clarkson again), Jesus just keeps piling it on.

"If your son fell into a well," he says, "or your ox, you'd pull them out, surely, Sabbath or not."

And once again – silence. 'Course they would. And they know it. And Jesus knows it too.

The hospitality quotient, however, has still shown no significant rise. So Jesus decides to tackle the issue "head-on". Hey, nobody else is talking, so he might as well take advantage of the opportunity.

He's noticed something, you see. These people can't even extend hospitality to each other. When they came in, they were jostling, pushing, even fighting for the best seats at the table.

Like punters rushing into a gig.

Like children grabbing for sweets.

Like gulls around a discarded bag of chips.

So he offers them a bit of advice. A short lesson on etiquette. On hospitality.

"When you're invited to dinner, don't plop your bottom down on the best seat. Because the host's favourite uncle, or his best mate, or his business partner, or someone he owes a shedload of money to, might come in after you. And he might want that seat for him. And that means you will have to suffer the embarrassment of being moved to a lesser perch.

"Better to perch yourself on that lesser seat first. And then enjoy that happy moment when your host calls across the room, 'My friend, what are you doing way over there? Come closer. Sit by me.'

"For those who exalt themselves will be humbled. And those who humble themselves will be lifted up."

It's quite possible that Jesus considers adding the odd application.

Something about religious leaders looking down on those who aren't as "good" as them, or looking carefully at those who don't quite share their theology. But the truth of the matter is that he gets distracted, for the longer Jesus looks back at the ones who are looking at him, the more clearly he sees the similarities among them. The same close-set eyes, the same right-angled cowlick, the same tilt to the nose. These men are related.

And like the royal families of Europe prior to the outbreak of the Great War, the inbreeding is obvious.

So he offers another little lesson on hospitality.

"When you throw a dinner party," he says, "don't invite your relatives, your neighbours and your rich friends. They'll just invite you back. And, in so doing, you'll be paid back.

"No, invite the poor, the lame, the blind. They can't pay you back, no way – but you will be blessed by their presence and repaid by God himself at the resurrection."

And then, finally, somebody speaks.

"Blessed is the man who will eat at the feast in the kingdom of God!" he says.

And it's hard to tell. Has this (by the standards of the rest of the company) loquacious guest made the connection between the resurrection and God's great eternal feast in heaven? Or has he, like Bertie Wooster in the absence of Jeeves, just blurted out the first thing that came into his slightly drunken head?

Whatever the case, Jesus leaps on this opportunity to say one last thing about hospitality. God's hospitality.

He tells them yet another story about a man who throws a banquet. When the meal is ready, he sends his servants round to collect the guests. But they're busy.

One is climbing the property ladder. One is becoming a cattle baron. And one is in the middle of his honeymoon.

So the servant goes back to the master and tells him that his guests won't be coming. And the master is furious. It's not that he has anything against estate agents or cows or nuptial bliss. It's just that he's put a lot of work into the feast, he's given plenty of notice, and these are (supposedly) his friends, and not the kind of people who invite you to dinner just to spy on you. (Jesus doesn't say that actually, but I think that's what he's getting at.)

So the man tells the servant to go out in the town and invite the poor, the sick and the lame (see above).

And when even they don't fill the table, he sends the servant out again to compel a crowd to come. ("You *will* come! You *will* eat! And you *will* clean your plate!" I always knew my mum had at least a few divine attributes.)

And as for the dinner guests who were too busy to come, the master says that none of them will ever taste his banquet.

Which would sound rather inhospitable, actually, had Jesus' hosts not already cornered that particular market.

Which is the point, actually. They know so little about hospitality that they can't even recognize it when it's handed to them.

Like on a plate.

Like on a platter.

At God's Great Feast.

Questions

1. Does this "hospitality" thing work, or are we grasping at straws here?

2. How would you describe God's hospitality?

3. I like the image of God's Big Feast. 'Cause I like to eat. Find other places in the Bible where God's grace or heaven are described in those terms.

A Lost Sheep

(Luke 15:1–7)

Introduction

I love the three "lost" stories, and the way they build.

One out of a hundred. One out of ten. One out of two. Or maybe two out of two. And God's grace there throughout. To rescue. To return. To save. Given the fact that they work together, I thought it would be fair to tell them in the same way. The Rhyming Way!

TELLING TIPS: See "Mary Meets an Angel" (above) for suggestions on how to tell this kind of story.

There once was a shepherd who had a hundred sheep.
There once was a shepherd who had a hundred sheep.
There once was a shepherd who had a hundred sheep.
They skipped and they frolicked and they leaped.
(Leap – even if just little!)
They skipped and they frolicked and they leaped.
They skipped and they frolicked and they leaped.

But one of the sheep was more curious than the rest,
But one of the sheep was more curious than the rest,
But one of the sheep was more curious than the rest,
And away from the others he creeped.
(Make a little creeping-away motion with hands.)
And away from the others he creeped.
And away from the others he creeped.

"Someone's missing," said the shepherd, when he counted up that night.
"Someone's missing," said the shepherd, when he counted up that night.
"Someone's missing," said the shepherd, when he counted up that night.
"Until I find him, I shall not go to sleep!"
(Head on hands, sleeping motion.)
"Until I find him, I shall not go to sleep!"
"Until I find him, I shall not go to sleep!"

So the shepherd left the ninety-nine and set off in the dark,
So the shepherd left the ninety-nine and set off in the dark,
So the shepherd left the ninety-nine and set off in the dark,
And behind every boulder he peeped.
(Peeping motion – hands above eyes.)
And behind every boulder he peeped.
And behind every boulder he peeped.

And finally he found him – that lost and lonely sheep,
And finally he found him – that lost and lonely sheep,
And finally he found him – that lost and lonely sheep,
Trapped in thorns, where the path was rough and steep.
(Pretend you're on the edge of a precipice, looking down, and frightened –
say "steep" with a little shriek.)
Trapped in thorns, where the path was rough and steep.
Trapped in thorns, where the path was rough and steep.

So the shepherd freed the sheep and set him on his shoulders.
So the shepherd freed the sheep and set him on his shoulders.
So the shepherd freed the sheep and set him on his shoulders.
"Man," he thought. "I sure could use a Jeep!"
(Pretend you are turning steering wheel.)
"Man," he thought. "I sure could use a Jeep!"
"Man," he thought. "I sure could use a Jeep!"

So the shepherd took the sheep and put him with the others,
So the shepherd took the sheep and put him with the others,
So the shepherd took the sheep and put him with the others,
In a white-and-woolly, happy-hundred heap.
(Make shape of heap with hands.)

In a white-and-woolly, happy-hundred heap.
In a white-and-woolly, happy-hundred heap.

Then the shepherd threw a party for his neighbours and his friends.
Then the shepherd threw a party for his neighbours and his friends.
Then the shepherd threw a party for his neighbours and his friends.
They skipped and they frolicked and they leaped.
(Repeat first motion.)
They skipped and they frolicked and they leaped.
They skipped and they frolicked and they leaped.

Questions

1. From what you know about sheep, is this "wandering away" thing normal behaviour?

2. Think or talk about a time when you wandered away.

3. How were you rescued? Did it cost anyone anything?

A Lost Coin

(Luke 15:8–10)

Introduction

See "A Lost Sheep" above.

> **TELLING TIPS: See "Mary Meets an Angel" (above) for
> suggestions on how to tell this kind of story.**

There once was a woman who had ten special coins.
There once was a woman who had ten special coins.
There once was a woman who had ten special coins.
They were silver. They were shiny. They were bright.
(Frame face with hands. Big smile.)
They were silver. They were shiny. They were bright.
They were silver. They were shiny. They were bright.

But one of the coins was smaller than the rest.
But one of the coins was smaller than the rest.
But one of the coins was smaller than the rest.
And it rolled away somewhere in the night.
(Sleep motion.)
And it rolled away somewhere in the night.
And it rolled away somewhere in the night.

"Something's missing," said the woman, when she looked into her purse.
"Something's missing," said the woman, when she looked into her purse.
"Something's missing," said the woman, when she looked into her purse.
And immediately she found herself a light.
(Switching on torch.)

And immediately she found herself a light.
And immediately she found herself a light.

So she switched on the light and grabbed herself a broom.
So she switched on the light and grabbed herself a broom.
So she switched on the light and grabbed herself a broom.
And she swept every corner in sight.
(Sweeping motion.)
And she swept every corner in sight.
And she swept every corner in sight.

Finally she found it, that lost and lonely coin.
Finally she found it, that lost and lonely coin.
Finally she found it, that lost and lonely coin.
In a crack where the floorboards were not tight.
(Hold hands tight together.)
In a crack where the floorboards were not tight.
In a crack where the floorboards were not tight.

Then the woman took the coin and put it with the rest.
Then the woman took the coin and put it with the rest.
Then the woman took the coin and put it with the rest.
"A cash machine," she thought, "would suit me right!"
(Motion – typing in PIN.)
"A cash machine," she thought, "would suit me right!"
"A cash machine," she thought, "would suit me right!"

Then the woman threw a party for her neighbours and her friends,
Then the woman threw a party for her neighbours and her friends,
Then the woman threw a party for her neighbours and her friends,
And they partied hard until it was daylight.
(Rub bleary eyes.)
And they partied hard until it was daylight.
And they partied hard until it was daylight.

And the angels party, too, when a sinner comes back home.
And the angels party, too, when a sinner comes back home.
And the angels party, too, when a sinner comes back home.

Angels silver. Angels shiny. Angels bright!
(Again frame face with hands and big smile.)
Angels silver. Angels shiny. Angels bright!
Angels silver. Angels shiny. Angels bright!

Questions

1. The coin, unlike the sheep, doesn't intentionally walk away. It just gets lost. Is there any significance to this, do you think? Or is that reading too much into the story?

2. Talk about a time when you lost something really important to you. Did you throw a party when you found it (assuming you did)? What was your reaction?

3. Do you feel the same way the woman did, the way the angels do, when someone comes to Jesus? Why or why not?

Lost Son

(Luke 15:11–32)

Introduction

See "A Lost Sheep" above.

> **TELLING TIPS: See "Mary Meets an Angel" (above) for suggestions on how to tell this kind of story. Oh, and in the "General Motors" section, the three different lines are unusual, but intentional. Just thought it was more fun that way!**

There once was a father who had a pair of sons.
There once was a father who had a pair of sons.
There once was a father who had a pair of sons.
One family, made up of three big guys!
(Make a strong-man motion or put arms around shoulders of people standing next to you.)
One family, made up of three big guys!
One family, made up of three big guys!

But one of the sons was less patient than the other.
But one of the sons was less patient than the other.
But one of the sons was less patient than the other.
"I want my money, Dad – can't wait for you to die."
(Make death motion – hanging, choking, or finger across throat – it's up to you!)
"I want my money, Dad – can't wait for you to die."
"I want my money, Dad – can't wait for you to die."

So the father gave the son his share of the estate,
So the father gave the son his share of the estate,
So the father gave the son his share of the estate,
And the son took off without saying goodbye.
(Wave goodbye.)
And the son took off without saying goodbye.
And the son took off without saying goodbye.

"I miss my boy," the father sighed, as he watched for him each day,
"I miss my boy," the father sighed, as he watched for him each day,
"I miss my boy," the father sighed, as he watched for him each day,
Eyes fixed on where the road met with the sky.
(Draw horizon line with finger.)
Eyes fixed on where the road met with the sky.
Eyes fixed on where the road met with the sky.

The son, meanwhile, burned through his cash, in a country far away.
The son, meanwhile, burned through his cash, in a country far away.
The son, meanwhile, burned through his cash, in a country far away.
He spent and spent like General Motors and the bills just piled up high.
(Raise hand up high.)
He spent and spent like an Investment Banker and the bills just piled up
   high.
He spent and spent like an MP on an expense account and the bills just
   piled up high.

Penniless and hungry, he found work at a local farm,
Penniless and hungry, he found work at a local farm,
Penniless and hungry, he found work at a local farm,
Chief Nutritional Technician in their top pigsty.
(Make snorting pig sound.)
Chief Nutritional Technician in their top pigsty.
Chief Nutritional Technician in their top pigsty.

"This is crazy," he decided. "I'd be better off back home."
"This is crazy," he decided. "I'd be better off back home."
"This is crazy," he decided. "I'd be better off back home."

And forthwith from that farm the son did fly!
(Flap arms like wings.)
And forthwith from that farm the son did fly!
And forthwith from that farm the son did fly!

And when, at last, the father saw his lost and lonely son,
And when, at last, the father saw his lost and lonely son,
And when, at last, the father saw his lost and lonely son,
He ran to him and hugged him and he cried.
(Trace imaginary tears down your cheeks.)
He ran to him and hugged him and he cried.
He ran to him and hugged him and he cried.

"My son was lost and now he's found! It's time to celebrate,
"My son was lost and now he's found! It's time to celebrate,
"My son was lost and now he's found! It's time to celebrate,
With a robe and a ring and a full-fat cow-child pie!
*(Pretend you're biting into a big piece of pie – you can use a pretend fork, if
    you like; I just hold it in my hand.)*
With a robe and a ring and a full-fat cow-child pie!
With a robe and a ring and a full-fat cow-child pie!

So the father threw a party for his neighbours and his friends,
So the father threw a party for his neighbours and his friends,
So the father threw a party for his neighbours and his friends,
And that was when the other son wandered by.
(Fingers walking in air.)
And that was when the other son wandered by.
And that was when the other son wandered by.

"What's going on?" he asked. And when he heard he cursed,
"What's going on?" he asked. And when he heard he cursed,
"What's going on?" he asked. And when he heard he cursed,
And, fuming, found his father and asked "Why?"
(Shrugging, palms up, "Why?" motion.)
And, fuming, found his father and asked "Why?"
And, fuming, found his father and asked "Why?"

"You've never thrown a party for me!" the son complained.
"You've never thrown a party for me!" the son complained.
"You've never thrown a party for me!" the son complained.
"And I do my best to please you – at least I try!"
(Swing arm in front of body, hand as fist.)
"And I do my best to please you – at least I try!"
"And I do my best to please you – at least I try!"

"What's mine is yours," the father said. "It's always been that way.
"What's mine is yours," the father said. "It's always been that way.
"What's mine is yours," the father said. "It's always been that way.
There's no need to rant or rage or even sigh.
(Sigh as you say "sigh".)
There's no need to rant or rage or even sigh.
There's no need to rant or rage or even sigh.

"But your brother's back, when he was gone. He was dead. Now he's
  alive.
"But your brother's back, when he was gone. He was dead. Now he's
  alive.
"But your brother's back, when he was gone. He was dead. Now he's
  alive.
We're a family again – We three big guys!"
(Repeat first motion.)
We're a family again – We three big guys!"
We're a family again – We three big guys!"

Questions

1. How is this story different from the previous two "lost" stories. How is it the same?

2. How would it change if it were told from the perspective of the son who stayed behind?

3. Why do you think Jesus told three "lost" stories and not just one?

Just Waiting

(Luke 15:11–32)

Introduction

Working on similar tellings of the three Lost stories got me thinking about their similarities and their differences. And also prompted the question that drives this piece.

Did you ever wonder why he didn't go?

Why he just stood there, waiting?

The shepherd went. He left the ninety-nine behind and went out in the country, went out all alone. He went, and he searched, until he found his lost sheep.

So why not the father? Why didn't he go? Why did he just stand there, waiting?

The woman went. Her coin was lost, so she lit a lamp, and grabbed a broom and went and swept and searched until she found her lost coin.

So why not the father? Why didn't he go? Why did he just stand there, waiting?

I think it's because there is a difference – a difference between a lost sheep and a lost coin and a lost son.

The sheep is unlikely to come home on its own. With some varieties of pigeon, and the odd Disney dog and cat, you have a chance. But a sheep? A sheep is not hard-wired to return to the pen. A sheep is more likely to get stuck, or slaughtered, or slip off a mountainside.

So you have to go out and find him.

Same with a coin. It's a rare bit of currency that leaps out of that crack in the floor, shouting, "I'm here! Look! Pick me up, please!"

Doesn't happen. Not in my experience. And, for the record, it's true of car keys, as well. You have to go out and find them.

But sons? Sons make choices. They decide to go away. And unless they decide to come back, there's not much point following them to that far country and dragging them home.

I think the father knew that. He knew that until his son was ready to make that choice – until he was fully and finally fed up with the path he had chosen – there was no point in trying to force him onto another path.

Mind you, I'm sure he wanted to. I bet it took every bit of energy just to stand there, every ounce of strength to wait, particularly on those days when his mind was occupied with the inevitable "what ifs?"

What if he's hurt?

What if he's in jail?

What if I had done something differently?

What if there is something I can do, today, now, to save him?

The "what ifs" and "the waiting" were just holding him there, in some kind of terrible tension, like an enormous rubber band, stretched near to breaking.

And maybe that is why, when his son finally appeared on the horizon, the father literally took off in his direction, robes flying, arms outstretched, the words hurtling out of his mouth: "You're back! You're alive! Welcome home!"

Because now there was something he could do.

Something more than waiting.

Questions

1. What do you think of my answer to the question the reading poses?

2. Was it cruel of the father to wait – if by going to the far country and acting, there was just the chance that he might have spared his son the humiliation and degradation that he suffered?

3. Have you ever found yourself in the tension that the father faced? How did you resolve that? Did you wait? Did you go? What happened?

Idol/Idle

(Matthew 16:13)

Introduction

Here's a little sketch about Mammon, and a few other idols. It simply reinforces Jesus' criticism of serving Mammon. In Psalm 96 and in the story about Elijah on Mount Carmel, the "gods of the nations" are made the subject of ridicule. The point is that, unlike Yahweh, who made the world, they can't actually do anything. They're idle! And so this sketch applies that same logic to a variety of other "idols" (both ancient and modern!).

> **TELLING TIPS: Read Psalm 96:1–5a and then go into the sketch. You will need people to play Mammon (who enters and kicks things off), Thor (who is already resting in his beach chair – do the horned-helmet-and-hammer thing for him), Posh (the pop idol, who sits in her beach chair, reading a magazine or doing her nails – you probably can't afford to buy what she would actually wear, so make do), Dawkins (the secular idol – he would look great in a monkey suit, or maybe even a monkey mask), and Baal (who is a voice off).**

(Read Psalm 96:1–5a.)

For all the gods of the nations are idols.
    They just sit there.
    Poles in the ground. Stones on a hill. Statues on a shelf.
    They can't do anything.
    They're idols.
    They're… idle.

156

(Mammon enters.)

Thor: Mammon, how's it going?

Mammon: Thor, good to see you, man *(sits down in spare beach chair)*. So what you been up to?

Thor: Nothing much. Doing that Valhalla thing. Hanging out with Odin and Loki – getting hammered mostly!

Mammon: Been a bit idle then?

Thor: You got it! And how about you? Been anywhere nice recently?

Mammon: Nah. You know what they say – "can't take me with you"! *(Looks around.)* So, uh, where are the regulars?

Thor: Away mostly. Ganesh, the elephant god, is on holiday. Saw him packing his trunk yesterday. And Buddha's off practising that one-hand-clapping thing again.

Mammon: So who's the new goddess?

Thor: Oh, that's Posh. Sort of a pop idol, if you get my drift.

Mammon: Looks familiar. Isn't she...?

Thor: Footballer's wife. That's right. In all the papers. Used to be in a kind of band, I think, but doesn't actually do very much now.

Posh: Can't be bovvered.

Mammon: A bit idle, then?

Thor: You got it!

Mammon: Listen, I can't stay long, but I – well, I need to use the toilet. Any chance?

Thor: Unlikely. Baal's in there again, and you know how long he takes. *(Turns and shouts:)* Baal! Mammon's here. He needs the loo! Oh, and there are 400 prophets desperate for your attention, as well. Something about a barbecue!

Baal: *(voice off)* I'll be out in a minute.

Thor: I bet he's got a paper.

Mammon: I bet he's got a magazine.

Posh: I bet he just can't be bovvered.

Mammon: And how about this guy over here? *(Thor goes to answer.)* No, wait, let me guess. Mahulawana, monkey god of the Toopa Toopa tribe.

Thor: Not even close.

Mammon:	Okay, how about Cheetah, divine protector of the Clan Burroughs?
Thor:	Miles off.
Mammon:	King Kong?
Thor:	Nope.
Mammon:	Curious George?
Thor:	*(sighs)* Look. Let me give you a little clue – he's a secular idol.
Mammon:	*(looks more closely)* Of course. Plain as the nose on my face. Ladies and gentlemen, taking a rest on the evolutionary highway – it's Richard Dawkins!
Richard Dawkins:	
	(Yelps and howls, monkey like.)
Mammon:	What he say?
Thor:	Something like, "That's right, you god-bothering imbecile. When are you going to recognize that man is the measure of all things?" Either that or he wants a banana.
Mammon:	Man. In control? Now that's a myth, if I ever heard one!
Thor:	Can't imagine it.
Posh:	Can't be bovvered.
Mammon:	Baal, listen, I'm desperate here! *(Looks down.)* And those prophets of yours are jumping around like they have to go, too!
Baal:	*(voice off – paper rustling)* I'm going as fast as I can!
Thor:	I'm telling you, he's not coming out. You might as well just wait till you get home. Look, his prophets have given up. And, yes, there on cue is Elijah, the prophet of You Know Who.
Mammon:	What, Voldemort?
Thor:	No, you know – the One!
Mammon:	What, Neo? I must say, while I enjoyed the first film, I was a bit confused by number three. I reckon that the CGI overwhelmed what little plot remained.
Thor:	No, not that One. *The* One. The One who does things. The One who makes things happen.
Mammon:	Oh, Him. I get exhausted just thinking about Him.
Thor:	You and me both.
Mammon:	Making the earth. That must have taken some doing.

Thor: Not to mention the sun.

Mammon: And the planets.

Thor: And the moon.

Mammon: And the stars.

Thor: And the rivers.

Mammon: And the mountains.

Posh: An' Essex, an' all.

Mammon: Yeah, well, it looks like he can start a fire, too. Elijah's little barbecue is a big hit with the crowd.

Thor: Does it ever make you jealous, though? Do you ever wish that we could do something like that?

Mammon: What? Like bring happiness? *(Sniggers.)* "Money Can't Buy Me Love", baby. That's what the song says, and that's what I'm sticking to. I mean, what would be the point of anything else? They worship us. And adore us. And sacrifice their lives and their stuff for us. And what do we have to do? Nothing. Just sit here. Sit here and be idle. Seems like a pretty good deal to me. Except, of course, *(towards the toilet)* WHEN YOU HAVE TO GO!

Thor: Is that music I hear in there? *(Gets up and looks off stage.)* Baal, did you take your iPod in with you?

Mammon: *(Gets up too.)* C'mon, Baal. It's been, what, a millennia or two? Give somebody else a chance!

Richard Dawkins:
            (Gets up as well – yelping and howling.)

Mammon: What he say?

Thor: Um, I think it was, "There is a real likelihood that Baal will ultimately emerge from the toilet. It may take a billion years, but given sufficient time and chance, any complex combination of outcomes is possible." Either that or he needs to make a whoopsie too.

Mammon: Well, his time is up and he's not getting any more chances. Baal, we're coming in! *(Heads off stage.)*

Richard Dawkins:
            (Follows, howling and yelping.)

Thor: Posh, are you coming? We need some help here.

Posh: *(Yawns – picks up a copy of* Hello!*)* Sorry. Call me idle, but I just can't be bovvered.

Questions

1. Are there any idols you would add to our cast?

2. Why do you think we worship idols when we have such an amazing God to worship instead?

3. Why is it impossible to serve both God and Mammon?

Lazarus and the Rich Man – an Introduction

(Luke 16:19–31)

Introduction

That's all this reading is. Literally. An introduction to the story of Lazarus and the Rich Man. I just think it's helpful to remind people, from time to time, that there is a thread, a consistent emphasis, that runs through the Gospel stories. In Luke it's the upside-down thing, the turning of the world on its head. It just keeps popping up, and knowing that helps us to understand each individual story and how it fits into the whole.

> **TELLING TIPS: Read the intro, then read the passage. Simple as that!**

It's one thing to hear it in your mother's womb:

> "He has filled the hungry with good things, but has sent the rich away empty."

It's another thing to preach it in your hometown:

> "Good news for the poor, freedom for the prisoners, recovery of sight for the blind."

Or enshrine it in words that will outlast generations:

> "Blessed are you who are poor, for your is the kingdom of God. Blessed are you who hunger now, for you will be satisfied."

But if you really want to make your point, I'm convinced that you need to tell it in a story:

> "There once was a rich man, dressed in purple, clothed in linen, living in the lap of luxury. And at his gate lay a beggar named Lazarus…"

Questions

1. Can you think of any other themes that run through the book of Luke – that keep coming up again and again?

2. What about Matthew or Mark or John?

3. Can you think of any other instances in the book of Luke where this reversal-of-roles thing also appears? Clue (and shameless plug) – have a look at "Kids, Camels and the Kingdom of God" in my previous book, *Telling the Bible.*

What Do You Want, a Personal Invitation?

(Luke 16:19–31)

Introduction

Jeremiah says something about the heart being deceitful above all things. I think what he means is that we can talk ourselves into anything, justify any behaviour, rationalize any decision. You know it, I know it, we all know it. Because we have all done it. The only things that change are the excuses. And this reading attempts to address at least one of them.

The rich man in the story is keen for Abraham to send Lazarus (Send Lazarus! As if he is still the poor beggar outside the gate and everybody's doormat, everybody's servant) to warn his brothers of what will happen if they do not change their ways.

Abraham's answer is clear. They have already been told what is right and what is wrong. It's there, for all to see, in the Law and the Prophets.

But the rich man is not satisfied. If someone were to come back from the dead, he argues, that would make a difference. It's an ironic suggestion, of course, coming from the mouth of Jesus, when Luke knows that is exactly what happened to him.

But Abraham's answer is the same. If they won't listen to the Law and the Prophets, how will a returning messenger from the dead make any difference?

And he's right, of course. God has given us all the information we need to know what's right and what's wrong. That's the first evidence of his grace. He doesn't keep us guessing – he shows us clearly which paths will lead to a good life and which will lead to destruction. And if we are obedient, then we don't need the next bit of his grace – his forgiveness (in that area, anyway).

The problem is – we want what we want. We want to do what we want to do. So we say that such and such doesn't seem wrong to us, or it's old-fashioned, or that's just how we are. Anything to do what we want. And the final recourse is: "Well, if X was really all that wrong, then God would have told me!"

The point of the story, of course, is that he has. It's right there – for all to read. We don't need a personal invitation.

TELLING TIPS: This is a two-hander. One reader tells the story and the other reader does the chorus/repetitive bit. I suppose you could also have the group read the chorus-y bit together.

"Look, I know the Bible says that what I'm doing is wrong. But, let's face it – it's an old book. So if God wants me to change, he's going to have to come and tell me himself."

Once upon a time there was a rich man, who lounged about in linen and lived in luxury. Outside his gate there lay a beggar named Lazarus, who longed to lick up what fell from the rich man's table.

"Look, I know the Bible says that what I'm doing is wrong. But, let's face it – it's an old book. So if God wants me to change, he's going to have to come and tell me himself."

Lazarus died, and was carried by the angels to Abraham's side. The rich man died, as well, and was carried away to hell.

"Look, I know the Bible says that what I'm doing is wrong. But, let's face it – it's an old book. So if God wants me to change, he's going to have to come and tell me himself."

Tormented by fire, the rich man looked up, and saw Lazarus and Abraham far away. "Help me, Father Abraham," he cried. "Have Lazarus dip his finger in the water and cool my burning tongue."

"Look, I know the Bible says that what I'm doing is wrong. But, let's face it – it's an old book. So if God wants me to change, he's going to have to come and tell me himself."

Abraham shook his ancient head. "When you were alive," he said, "You had everything you wanted. Lazarus had nothing. Now he lives in luxury, and you are the one in pain. And besides, there is a gulf between us, fixed, and deep, and impossible to cross. There is nothing he can do."

"Look, I know the Bible says that what I'm doing is wrong. But, let's face it – it's an old book. So if God wants me to change, he's going to have to come and tell me himself."

"Then, if he cannot come to me," the rich man cried, "send him to my father's house. Send him to warn my brothers, so that they will not have to suffer this pain."

"Look, I know the Bible says that what I'm doing is wrong. But, let's face it - it's an old book. So if God wants me to change, he's going to have to come and tell me himself."

Again Abraham shook his head. "They already have Moses and the Prophets," he said, "to tell them all that God requires. Let your brothers listen to them."

"Look, I know the Bible says that what I'm doing is wrong. But, let's face it – it's an old book. So if God wants me to change, he's going to have to come and tell me himself."

"But if someone comes back from the dead," the rich man cried, "someone sent by God to speak to them directly, surely then they will repent."

"Look, I know the Bible says that what I'm doing is wrong. But, let's face it – it's an old book. So if God wants me to change, he's going to have to come and tell me himself."

And a third time, Abraham shook his ancient head. "If they won't listen to Moses and the Prophets," he said, "They are unlikely to be convinced, even if someone should come to them from the dead."

"Look, I know the Bible says that what I'm doing is wrong. But, let's face it – it's an old book. So if God wants me to change, he's going to have to come and...oh, I see. He already has."

Questions

1. Is this too hard a line to take?

2. Can you think of a time when you talked yourself into doing something you knew was wrong? Or rationalized some wrong act?

3. Is knowing what is right all that is necessary for doing what is right? What else is required? What part does knowledge play?

This Story is Brought to You by the Letter T

(Luke 17:11–19)

Introduction

I do this as a "number" story in *The Lion Storyteller Bible*. So I figured "letters" would make a nice change of pace.

TELLING TIPS:
- **Travelling – pretend walking, swinging arms**
- **Town – trace shape of a few buildings with finger**
- **Ten – ten fingers in air (be grateful we're not doing the twelve disciples!)**
- **Terribly – shudder**
- **Trust – hand on heart**
- **Turned – turn around or turn to side**
- **Thank you – both hands extended in a thanking gesture, or a thumbs up**
- **Threw – pretend to throw something to the ground**
- **Touched – drag finger down cheek like tear**

As with the other Letter Stories, teach your group the key words and their actions/sounds before you do the story, then lead them in the actions when you reach the appropriate points.

So Jesus was Travelling.
Travelling along the border that ran between Galilee and Samaria.

And as he Travelled, he came to a Town.

In the Town, there were Ten men. Ten men with leprosy. Some Jewish. Some Samaritan. Strange how contagion makes good bedfellows.

"We are Terribly, Terribly ill," they called to him, from a distance. "Have pity on us, please."

So Jesus honoured their Trust.

"Go. Show yourselves to a priest," he said. It was the lawful thing to do, to prove that you were no longer a risk to others.

So off they Travelled. And as they went, they were healed.

We don't know what happened to the others, but one of the men Turned around and ran back to Jesus.

"Thank you!" he cried.

And he Threw himself at Jesus' feet.

"Ten men," said Jesus. "And only one came back to say Thank you. And wouldn't you know it? He's a Samaritan. A foreigner."

Jesus was Touched. "Rise up and go," he smiled. "Your faith has made you well."

So off he went. One out of Ten. One out of Ten who said Thank you.

Questions

1. So what's the point of this story? The healing? The foreigner? Both?

2. Why do you suppose the others failed to come back? Was it simply ingratitude, or might there have been other reasons? Like what, do you think?

There Was an Old Woman Who Pestered a Judge

(Luke 18:1–8)

Introduction

I really got a kick out of writing (and performing) this one. The story of the Persistent Woman and the Unjust Judge is one of those more puzzling narratives and one, therefore, that doesn't seem to get addressed that often. I simply wanted to get across the idea of persistence – the never-ending nagging that Jesus suggests she used to get the judge to vindicate her. And that's when the song popped into my head – "There was an old woman who swallowed a fly…"

I cheated a bit, I must admit. "Pudge" is a little forced. It's short for "pudginess", of course – and I suspect she lost it due to her incessant activity and worrying (a point I made when I reached that verse and needed a breath).

Feel free to comment along the way – it just gets more and more ridiculous, and that's all part of the fun.

> **TELLING TIPS: Sing to the tune of "There Was an Old Woman Who Swallowed a Fly". You can put the words on a screen, but I found that folks gave up after a while and I was on my own anyway. It does need a lot of practice to work well – and at speed.**

There was an old woman who pestered a judge
To keep from her record a character smudge,
But he wouldn't budge.

There was an old woman who niggled and nudged.
I don't know why she niggled and nudged.
She niggled and nudged to pester a judge
To keep from her record a character smudge,
But he wouldn't budge.

There was an old woman who tramped and trudged.
I don't know why she tramped and trudged.
She tramped and trudged to niggle and nudge.
She niggled and nudged to pester a judge
To keep from her record a character smudge,
But he wouldn't budge.

There was an old woman who slipped on the sludge.
I don't know why she slipped on the sludge.
She slipped on the sludge as she tramped and trudged.
She tramped and trudged to niggle and nudge.
She niggled and nudged to pester a judge
To keep from her record a character smudge,
But he wouldn't budge.

There was an old woman whose life was a drudge.
I don't know why her life was a drudge.
Her life was a drudge 'cause she slipped on the sludge.
She slipped on the sludge as she tramped and trudged.
She tramped and trudged to niggle and nudge.
She niggled and nudged to pester a judge
To keep from her record a character smudge,
But he wouldn't budge.

There was an old woman who harboured a grudge.
I don't know why she harboured a grudge.
She harboured a grudge 'cause her life was a drudge.
Her life was a drudge 'cause she slipped on the sludge.
She slipped on the sludge as she tramped and trudged.
She tramped and trudged to niggle and nudge.
She niggled and nudged to pester a judge

To keep from her record a character smudge,
But he wouldn't budge.

There was an old woman who lost all her pudge.
I don't know why she lost all her pudge.
She lost all her pudge 'cause she harboured a grudge.
She harboured a grudge 'cause her life was a drudge.
Her life was a drudge 'cause she slipped on the sludge.
She slipped on the sludge as she tramped and trudged.
She tramped and trudged to niggle and nudge.
She niggled and nudged to pester a judge
To keep from her record a character smudge,
But he wouldn't budge.

There was an old woman who swallowed some fudge.
I don't know why she swallowed that fudge.
She swallowed the fudge 'cause she lost all her pudge.
She lost all her pudge 'cause she harboured a grudge.
She harboured a grudge 'cause her life was a drudge.
Her life was a drudge 'cause she slipped on the sludge.
She slipped on the sludge as she tramped and trudged.
She tramped and trudged to niggle and nudge.
She niggled and nudged to pester a judge
To keep from her record a character smudge,
But he wouldn't budge.

"I'm tired of this song, now," complained the judge,
"And tired of that woman (what's her name?), Miss Margery Mudge."
She swallowed the fudge 'cause she lost all her pudge.
She lost all her pudge 'cause she harboured a grudge.
She harboured a grudge 'cause her life was a drudge.
Her life was a drudge 'cause she slipped on the sludge.
She slipped on the sludge as she tramped and trudged.
She tramped and trudged to niggle and nudge.
She niggled and nudged to pester a judge
To keep from her record a character smudge.
"So at last I'll budge!"

Questions

1. What is the point of the story, do you think?

2. Is God like the unjust judge? Or is Jesus doing a bit of contrasting here?

3. Does persistence in prayer mean that we will always get what we want? Experience does not suggest so. So is it more likely that "persistence" and "vindication" are the key words here?

Two Men in a Temple

(Luke 18:9–14)

Introduction

Some passages just lend themselves to certain kinds of retellings. This one breaks up nicely into two. I thought that alternating the characters would help to emphasize the differences between them.

> **TELLING TIPS: Another two-hander – for you and another reader. You can also put the text up on a screen, divide the group in two and lead them in the readings. And if you do it that way, then they could even "act out" their parts (which I have suggested in parentheses with each line).**

Pharisee: A Pharisee went to the temple to pray.

Tax collector: And a tax collector went there, too.

Pharisee: The Pharisee stood up. *(Stand up.)*

Tax collector: The tax collector stood far away. *(Take a step back or to the side.)*

Pharisee: The Pharisee prayed about himself. *(Points to self.)*

Tax collector: The tax collector would not even lift his eyes to heaven. *(Look down.)*

Pharisee: "Thank you, God," the Pharisee prayed, "that I am not like other people." *(Lift hands to heaven.)*

Tax collector: The tax collector beat his breast. *(Beat breast.)*

Pharisee: "Like thieves," the Pharisee continued. *(Point to imaginary thief.)*

Tax collector: "God, have mercy," prayed the tax collector. *(Look down.)*

Pharisee: "Like sinners." *(Point to imaginary sinners.)*

Tax collector: "God, have mercy." *(Look down, get quieter.)*

Pharisee:	"'Like adulterers." *(Point to imaginary adulterer.)*
Tax collector:	"God, have mercy." *(Look down, get quieter still.)*
Pharisee:	"Or even like that tax collector over there." *(Point to tax collector.)*
Tax collector:	"God, have mercy." *(Look down, really quiet.)*
Pharisee:	"Twice a week I fast, and I tithe everything I get." *(Point to self, proudly.)*
Tax collector:	"God have mercy on me, a sinner." *(Point to self, sadly.)*
All:	I tell you that it was the tax collector, and not the Pharisee, who went home vindicated by God. For he who lifts himself up will be humbled, and he who humbles himself will be lifted up.

Questions

1. Can you think of a time when you approached God like the Pharisee?

2. How about the tax collector?

3. In what way, exactly, is the Pharisee an example of self-righteousness?

And Jesus Was Sad

(Luke 18:18–25)

Introduction

As promised, this is a companion piece to the earlier "And Jesus Was Confused" reading. Did Jesus ask people who wanted to follow him to change? Of course he did. And in this case, it was even a precondition, because of the hold this particular man's temptation had on his life.

> **TELLING TIPS: This is one to read on your own. Read the passage of Scripture up to the point where Jesus tells the man to give up his treasure to the poor, then follow with the reading below.**

And the rich young ruler said, "Hang on a minute! You want me to change? Now?

"The buzz on the street is that you're all about 'acceptance'. That we're all on a journey. That change comes, I don't know, gradually, down the line, tomorrow, next month, next year, some place shortly before that final breath. But now? You want me to change, just like that? Now?"

Jesus opened his mouth to answer, but the rich young ruler was on a roll.

"I mean. This thing. This 'riches' thing that you so casually dismiss. This is who I am! I was born this way!

"No, I mean it. Literally. My dad was wealthy. His dad before him. And the minute I was born, there were trust funds with my name on them. Set for life. Sorted. And you just want me to give that up? Now?

"It's a kind of prejudice, isn't it? Admit it. You're a poor rabbi and you just can't stand the idea that someone could be different from you. Follow

God and still be rich. Well, there are lots of us about. I want you to know that. We may be a minority, but we're a significant minority, and this fencing-off, this prejudice, this... this... phobia of yours is obviously just some peculiar, private, judgmental way of excluding people who are not like you."

Jesus opened his mouth again...

"How dare you? I mean, how dare you? How dare you judge me just because I'm different? It's not my fault that I'm wealthy, and I'm not going to apologize to anyone for how I am. In fact, I'm not so sure I even want to follow you any more! How about that?

"Why should I pay attention to someone who can't accept even the most basic, fundamental thing about me? There are rabbis, perfectly good rabbis, who wouldn't bat any eyelash at my money. Who would embrace it, in fact. So maybe I'll just go and talk to one of them. How about that? And then you can go and nurse your prejudice and live in your intolerant little world with your intolerant little friends.

"Change? Now? Ridiculous!"

And the rich young ruler turned and walked away.

And Jesus? The Bible says that Jesus was very sad.

Questions

1. Is the church actually more interested in personal change than Jesus was?

2. How do acceptance and transformation work together?

3. Why was Jesus so keen that the man give his money away before he followed him?

He was a Rich Man

(Luke 18:18–25; 19:1–10)

Introduction

Sometimes it helps to look at two stories together. It gives you a better idea of what each of them is about.

> **TELLING TIPS: Two readers again – sometimes together, sometimes separately.**

A & B: He was a rich man.

A & B: He was looking for Jesus.

A: So he walked up to Jesus, one day.

B: So he crept out of his house, one day.

A: And he asked Jesus a question.

B: And he climbed up a tree.

A & B: He was a rich man.

A & B: He was looking for Jesus.

A: Everyone respected him.

B: Everyone despised him.

A: Because he was so good at being good.

B: Because he was so good at being bad – a tax collector, a traitor, and a cheat.

A & B: He was a rich man.

A & B: He was looking for Jesus.

A: "What must I do, Jesus," he asked, "to inherit eternal life?"

B: "What should I do?" he wondered. "If the crowd spots me here, I could lose my life."

A: "You know the law," Jesus answered. "No adultery. No murder. No stealing. No lying. Honour your dad and your mum."

B: "I need somewhere to eat," Jesus announced. "Where shall I go for my tea?"

A & B: He was a rich man.

A & B: He was looking for Jesus.

A: "I have done all those things since I was a boy," the rich man said.

B: "There's no reason he'd want to come to my house," the rich man sighed.

A: "Then there's just one thing you lack," said Jesus, looking him in the eye. "Sell all you have and give it to the poor. Then come and follow me."

B: "Come down!" said Jesus, looking up through the leaves. "I'm staying at your house today."

A & B: He was a rich man.

A & B: He was looking for Jesus.

A: And the rich man looked down at the ground.

B: And the rich man climbed down from the tree.

A: And the rich man was very sad.

B: And the rich man was very glad.

A: And the rich man declined the offer.

B: And the rich man came up with an offer – half his possessions to the poor, and four times back what he had stolen.

A: And Jesus said, "How hard it is for the rich to enter the kingdom. It's easier for a camel to go through the eye of a needle than for a rich man to enter the kingdom of God."

B: And Jesus said, "Today salvation has come to this house, because this man too is a son of Abraham. For the Son of Man came to seek and to save what was lost."

A & B: He was a rich man.

A & B: He was looking for Jesus.

Questions

1. There is no way of knowing what Jesus and Zacchaeus talked about over dinner, but, given the result, do you think that the conversation bore any resemblance to the chat he had with the rich ruler?

2. Why do you think the two rich men responded differently?

3. What did Jesus mean when he said that Zacchaeus was a son of Abraham?

Noisy Beggar

(Luke 18:35–43)

Introduction

This is another one of those persistence stories, isn't it? I suppose I could have done another song – "There was a Blind Beggar Who Sat by the Road". But I thought this would work better, and get the idea of the man's persistent (and noisy) nature across just as well.

> **TELLING TIPS: Divide your group into three parts. Teach them the line, "Jesus, Son of David, have mercy on me" – and then lead them in shouting that line each time you point at their group. I have made it easier by putting a group number before each line and also ensuring that the line comes three times each time it appears.**
>
> **To make things more interesting, you could have the first group shout at one level, group 2 more loudly, and group 3 loudest of all. Warn small children this is happening, though. Some of them really hate loud noises.**
>
> **Notice that there is a slight change of tense the final time they do their lines – but I have given you the line as well, so you have the opportunity to make that clear.**

As Jesus came near to Jericho, a blind man sat by the roadside. He sat there begging.

He heard the crowd go by. And so he asked someone what was going on.

"It's Jesus of Nazareth," they told him. "He's coming this way."

So the blind man cried, (1) "Jesus, Son of David, have mercy on me!"

Then he did it again. (2) "Jesus, Son of David, have mercy on me!"

And again. (3) "Jesus, Son of David, have mercy on me!"

"Quiet!" said the crowd.

"Settle down."

"Shut up."

But the more they shouted at him, the louder he shouted back.

(1) "Jesus, Son of David, have mercy on me!"

(2) "Jesus, Son of David, have mercy on me!"

(3) "Jesus, Son of David, have mercy on me!"

So Jesus stopped...

(1) "Jesus, Son of David, have mercy on me!"

and ordered the man...

(2) "Jesus, Son of David, have mercy on me!"

to be brought to him.

(3) "Jesus, Son of David, have mercy on me!"

And when he arrived...

(1) "Jesus, Son of David, have mercy on me!"

Jesus asked him...

(2) "Jesus, Son of David, have mercy on me!"

"What do you want..."

(3) "Jesus, Son of David, have mercy on me!"

"me to do for you?"

"Oh," said the man, once the shouting had stopped. "That's better. I want you to make me see again."

So Jesus did.

"You can see now," he said. "Your faith has made you well."

And when Jesus left, the man followed him, praising God as he went. Blind no more. But noisy as ever. And operating in a slightly different tense.

"Jesus, Son of David *had* mercy on me!"

(1) "Jesus, Son of David had mercy on me!"

(2) "Jesus, Son of David had mercy on me!"

(3) "Jesus, Son of David had mercy on me!"

Questions

1. Why do you think the crowd rebuked the man and told him to be quiet? It's not like they were in the library or at the cinema.

2. Why do you think the man was so persistent?

3. And why do you think Jesus asked him what he wanted?

The Taxman's Tale

(Luke 19:1–10)

Introduction

Nobody likes to pay taxes. But when the taxes go to an oppressive government you never voted for, and when the tax collector charges far more than he should just to line his own pocket, then it makes paying taxes that much harder to bear.

That's how it was in Palestine, where Jesus lived. The Jewish people were ruled by the Romans, who had conquered them many years earlier. And their taxes went, not only to support their conquerors, but also to enrich the local tax collectors – fellow Jews who profited by collaborating with the Romans.

Tax collectors, therefore, were "the bad guys". And you can understand why they were hated and despised and lumped, by polite society, with the lowest of the low. Jesus didn't look at it that way, however. He spent a lot of his time with folk who were considered "bad", and he received his share of criticism for that. But he kept on doing it, all the same, because he believed that no one was out of reach of God's forgiveness and life-changing love. Not even greedy tax collectors – like Zacchaeus.

TELLING TIPS: This is one to tell on your own.

He loved the sound of coins.

The ringing and the jingling as they rained out of his cupped hand.

The clicking and the clacking as they struck the wooden table.

And the soft "shoop-shoop" as he slid each one into its pile.

He loved the sound of coins. So there was no better time than counting time. And his servants had strict instructions that he was to be left alone, in peace and in quiet – instructions that they were more than willing to keep, for he was a hard and a miserable master, even at the best of times.

Drop a cup, or rattle a pot, or – heaven forbid! – break a bowl or a pitcher, and an angry *"Quiet!"* would echo from the counting room. And so his servants tiptoed around the house at this time of day, terrified of making even the slightest noise.

Their fear and their anxiety meant nothing to him, however. They were, after all, no more than coins as far as he was concerned.

Five coins for the cook.

Two for the maid.

And one for the boy who minded his donkey.

And names? What was the point of learning names? They never stayed that long. And, anyway, it was the coins, the coins that counted.

The coins he took from the citizens of Jericho.

The coins he passed on to the Roman Government.

And, most important of all, the coins he kept for himself!

That was the sum total of the tax collector's life. As for multiplying friendships, well, that was simply not prudent. For friends would only use the relationship to wriggle out of their obligation. And adding acquaintances? That was no more likely. For what time was left when the collecting and the counting was done? And who would want to be seen with a Roman collaborator, anyway?

No. Taking away the hard-earned money of Jericho, and dividing the piles between himself and the Romans – those were the functions that mattered. And the coins. The sound of counting coins.

But, one day, there came another sound. An invading sound. The sound of laughter and cheering and crowds. And the tax collector was quick to react.

"Quiet!" he shouted. But the sound did not go away.

"Quiet, I said!" he shouted more loudly. And still the sound would not cease.

"Quiet!" he shouted a third time, as loudly as he could, banging his fist on the table and sending a tingling quiver through the coins. *"Quiet! I need quiet!"*

At last, the door creaked open, and a frightened whisper crept into the counting room.

"We're very sorry, master, but there is nothing we can do about the noise. It's coming from the street."

"Then clear the rabble away!" the taxman growled. "I have work to do. I need quiet."

"But, sir," the voice pleaded, "it's not just a few people. Everyone is out there. Everyone in Jericho!'

"Another holiday, I suppose," groaned the tax collector. Then he launching into a tirade that the servant had heard a hundred times before.

"These people – they complain about paying their taxes. 'It's a day's wage!' they moan. 'How will we feed our families?' But give them a holiday, and they'll gladly lose a day's wage – the hypocrites!"

"But it's not a holiday, sir," the servant answered. "It's Jesus. The teacher and miracle-worker. Jesus is coming to town!"

The tax collector groaned again. If there was one thing he hated more than noise, it was religion. It wasn't just the long list of rules – the do's and don'ts that would put any self-respecting taxman out of business. No, it was the money.

A coin for the priest.

A coin for the temple.

A coin for the sacrifice.

A coin for the poor.

And soon there were no coins left!

Again, he just couldn't understand the hypocrisy. The people hated him for what he took, but they were glad to give up a tenth of what they earned – and more! – so that priests, who were already fatter than him, could grow fatter still.

"I have no time for religion!" the taxman shouted. "I have work to do!"

"Ah, but Jesus is different," said the servant, thinking fast and hoping to win a little favour. "They say he's the friend of tax collectors!"

"The friend of tax collectors?" sneered the taxman. "That'll be the day!" And he slammed the door shut, nearly smashing his servant's nose.

And yet… and yet… and yet, as he sat there and counted, the taxman's curiosity grew.

"A religious teacher *and* the friend of tax collectors?" he wondered. "How exactly does that work?" And then the tax collector grinned. For the first time in a long time, a mischievous smile found its way onto his face.

"Blessed are the shaker-downers," he chuckled. "And the rougher-uppers, and the over-chargers, and the bottom-liners. Blessed are the tax collectors!" he cheered. And at that moment, he made up his mind. He would leave his counting for the moment. He would venture out into the street. He would go and see this Jesus!

Now don't be mistaken. This was not a rash decision. As with everything else in his life, he counted the cost carefully. If he was spotted, he would certainly be cursed or spat upon or possibly even attacked by some angry taxpayer he'd overcharged or by some political fanatic who resented his connections with the Roman overlords. But a quick peep out of the window assured him that everyone's attention was turned to the street. So who would notice if someone – particularly someone small of stature like himself – were to sneak quietly behind the crowd and have a look?

And that's just what the tax collector did. He locked up his coins and he crept out the door and he picked his way carefully along the back of the crowd. But it wasn't long before he realized that there was one part of the equation he had not taken into account: smallness was good for sneaking. Smallness was good for creeping. Smallness was especially good for not being seen. But as far as seeing was concerned, smallness was no good at all!

Yes, he could have wriggled and squirmed his way through the crowd. But that would have been unwise. For there, in that gap, was the broad backside of Benjamin the butcher, who had threatened him with a very sharp knife the last time that taxes were due. And in the next gap were the unmistakably flat feet of shepherd Baruch – feet that had found their way to the taxman's bottom a time or two. And over there? Well, what did it matter? The crowd was packed with people he had deceived or cheated or overcharged.

And then he saw it, standing tall at the end of the street. A single sycamore tree, with branches broad enough and full enough to conceal a small and nervous tax collector. And just high enough to give him a perfect view.

So over he crept and up he climbed, and because the crowd was so keen to see Jesus, no one noticed him. No one at all.

The tax collector, however, could see everything. There was Jesus, or at least that's who he assumed it was, greeting the cheering crowd. And there were the town dignitaries, of course, the rich and respected ones, pushing their way to the front. He knew what they were saying, even though he was too far away to hear:

"Come to my house, Jesus!"

"Eat at my table, Jesus!"

"Visit my home, Jesus!"

There was nothing hospitable about this, of course. Each and every one of those hypocrites was just anxious to hear the "Ooohs" and "Aaahs" of the crowd when this famous holy man agreed to honour their house with his presence.

But as the tax collector watched, the most remarkable thing began to happen. With every greeting, with every request, Jesus gently shook his head – "No, thank you."

"Is he leaving town so quickly?" the tax collector wondered. "Or has he already made some other arrangements? If not, he had better make up his mind soon, for he's almost at the end of the street."

And, at that very moment, Jesus stopped. And looked up. And spoke one word and one word only.

"Zacchaeus."

The tax collector hardly knew what to do. He thought he was hidden. He thought he was safe. And besides, it had been so long since he'd heard his name spoken, it hardly seemed as if it belonged to him at all. The servants called him "Sir", and the townspeople had their own selection of names for him. And as for anybody else… well, there wasn't anybody else. Not until now, anyway.

"Zacchaeus!" Jesus called again. "Zacchaeus, come down!"

And with that the crowd began to mock and to point and to howl. "The tax collector! Look! The tax collector is up in the tree!" But their laughter collapsed into stunned silence at Jesus' final words.

"Zacchaeus," he said again, "I'm coming to your house, today."

Leaves. Leaves against leaves – that was the only sound, as Zacchaeus climbed slowly down the tree. But with each branch, a new thought went racing through his head:

"Why is Jesus doing this?"

"Is this some kind of trick?"

"What will the people do?"

and "Is there anything in the pantry?"

It had been ages since anyone had visited his home, so Zacchaeus simply muttered, "Come this way," and hoped that he could remember what to do. As for the crowd, their surprise soon turned into something uglier.

"He's a thief! He's a cheat! He's a sinner!" the crowd complained. "Why is Jesus eating with him?" Part of it was jealousy. And part of it was confusion. Holy men ate with good people – that's what they were used to.

But this was different. And in that difference lay the explanation for what happened next.

Maybe it had to do with what Jesus said. Or maybe with what he did. Or maybe it was no more than Jesus' willingness to call Zacchaeus by name and offer to be his friend. But when dinner was over, Zacchaeus came out of his house again, not creeping, not sneaking, but standing tall (or at least as tall as he was able!).

"I have something to say to you," he announced to the crowd. "Something to say to you all. I'm sorry. I'm sorry for cheating you and deceiving you and making myself rich at your expense." And then he waved his hand and his servants came out of the house, as well, carrying bags of coins.

"My life was all about taking away. But from now on, that will be different. Half of all I own, I give to the poor. And whatever I have stolen from anyone, I will multiply by four and return to them, here and now."

Someone gasped. Someone shouted. And soon the whole crowd cheered.

"Salvation has come to this house!" cheered Jesus along with them. But as Zacchaeus tore open the money bags and his fortune spilled out through his fingers, all he could hear were the coins, the beautiful sound of the coins, ringing and jingling – and given away!

Questions

See the previous reading.

This Story is Brought to You by the Letter C

(Luke 19:28–40)

Introduction

I'm growing fond of this little storytelling device.

> **TELLING TIPS:** As with G, teach your group the sounds/actions to go with the key words beforehand. The more fun you have teaching them, the more they will enjoy doing them!
>
> - **Colt** – donkey hee-haw sound, hands flapping for ears
> - **Confrontation** – turn to neighbour and raise fists, boxing style
> - **Cloak** – pretend to pull off jumper, or, if appropriate, actually do it
> - **Crowd** – make "rhubarb" noises
> - **Cheer** – obviously
> - **Complaining** – grumbling noises
> - **Chuckle** – obvious, once again
> - **Cry out** – That's a tricky one – maybe a little raspy voice, tight-lipped kind of thing (like you're a stone) – "Go, Jesus!"

It starts off with a *colt*.

"Bring me one," Jesus tells his disciples. "The colt of an ass. One that has never been ridden."

It continues with a potential *confrontation*.

"If anyone asks you why you're taking the colt," says Jesus, "tell them the Lord needs it."

So they take the colt. And they get asked. And the owners seem satisfied with the answer.

And then there are the *cloaks*.

The disciples put their cloaks on the colt.

They put Jesus on the cloaks.

And as the colt clip-clops along, there are more cloaks, spread by the people on the road before it.

And they wave palms (though Luke doesn't actually mention it), lots of palms.

A *crowd* gathers.

At the top of the Mount of Olives.

And they *cheer*.

Praising God for his miracles, they shout, "Blessed is the king who comes in the name of the Lord! Peace in heaven and glory in the highest!"

And then the Pharisees arrive, *complaining*!

Things are getting out of hand. This looks like a coronation to them. It smells of Messiah. They don't like it and they reckon the Romans won't either. So they tell Jesus to tell off his disciples.

But Jesus just *chuckles*.

"Tell you what," he says, "even if I could shut them up, the stones would *cry out* in their place!"

See? (C?)

Questions

1. So what's going on here? Why all the palaver with colts and cloaks? What's Jesus up to?

2. And why are the Pharisees so upset?

3. And why do we celebrate this particular event?

Too Much

(Luke 21:1–4)

Introduction

Sometimes it's interesting to find out how little you need to say to tell a story. I think you'd need to know it to get this – but still, I think we get there.

> **TELLING TIPS: Read the passage. Do the reading. Maybe have your group do it with you.**

Too long
Too far
To Temple
Too much.

Too old
Too weak
Too weary
Too much.

Too sad
Too poor
Too lonely
Too much.

Two coins
Two left
To give
Too much!

Questions

1. Too short? What might you add?

2. Have you ever given the last you had of something? What was that like?

3. What does this story say about Jesus' understanding of both the rich and the poor? About his attitude towards giving?

The Lovin' God Party – a Song

(Matthew 22:34–40)

Introduction

Here's a happy little song about the greatest commandment. Feel free to replace the names, if there's someone you think fits better.

TELLING TIPS: Yes, there are actions. Inevitably.

First line
Heart – point to heart, or hold hands over heart
Soul – point to shoe (sole – get it?)
Mind – point to head
Body – shake body

Second line – little twist dance move

Third line – same as first

Fourth line – point to neighbour, point to self

Heart and Soul and Mind and Body,
Every bit invited to the "Lovin' God Party".
Heart and Soul and Mind and Body,
Love your neighbour as you love yourself.

Love him with your heart – like Mother Theresa.
Love him with your soul – like the Revd Al Green.
Love him with your mind – like C. S. Lewis.
Love him with your bodies – do the dancin' thing!

Heart and Soul and Mind and Body,
Every bit invited to the "Lovin' God Party".
Heart and Soul and Mind and Body,
Love your neighbour as you love yourself.

Questions

1. What does it mean to love God with your heart?

2. With your soul?

3. With your mind and body?

The Traitor's Tale

(Luke 22:1–6)

Introduction

So why did he do it? Why did Judas betray Jesus? People have been asking that question ever since those thirty pieces of silver changed hands.And they have come up with a lot of different answers.

Some have suggested that even though Judas was a follower of Jesus – one of his twelve disciples – he simply misunderstood what Jesus was all about. Others have pointed to the money. Or to the influence of the devil. And some have argued that the reason was political – that Judas was originally part of a revolutionary movement that wanted to overthrow the Romans and believed that Jesus would help that cause. And that the betrayal was a result of Judas's frustration when he realized that was not Jesus' intent at all. Finally, there are those who suggest that it was all somehow God's fault – that someone had to do the deed and it was Judas's fate to be the one.

As you will see in the following story, I think there is a case to be made for some of these arguments. Except for the last one, that is.

Judas made a decision. He may have been tempted to do it. But he was not forced. Not by God. Not by fate. Not by anyone. His motives may have been pure, they may have been selfish, they may have been confused. But the inescapable fact is this: regardless of Judas's reason for betraying Jesus, that betrayal resulted in Jesus' death.

TELLING TIPS: This is one to tell on your own.

"He's just not practical!" moaned Judas. "I think my objection boils down, basically, to that."

Judas's companion nodded his head, sympathetically. "I can see your problem," he said. "The man is unfamiliar with the ways of the world."

"Exactly!" Judas agreed, banging his hand on the table. "I knew you would understand." The disciple liked this man. He was a minor official on the temple staff – the assistant to the assistant to the assistant of the High Priest, or something like that. Judas had met him quite by chance, but they had "clicked" almost at once. The man was articulate, confident, poised. And best of all, he seemed to sympathize with the disciple's ever-growing frustration.

"Lofty sentiments. High ideals," the companion went on. "But it takes more than that to change the world, doesn't it?"

"It's what I've been saying for years." The disciple sighed. "But no one wants to listen. Least of all him! We need a power-base, I argue. We need to solidify our following. We need a realistic plan…"

"You need money," added the companion.

"Money!" the disciple sighed again. "Don't talk to me about money. Talk to him! He treats it like it was leprosy! No, I take that back – he treats lepers better than he treats your average rich man."

The companion leaned forward, intrigued. "How so?"

Judas sighed. "Where do I start? There are so many examples. All right, here's one:

"This fellow comes along, one day. He's rich – it's obvious. His clothes. His jewellery. The way he walks and holds his head. He wants to join up with us, so he asks Jesus what he has to do. No, no, first he calls Jesus 'Good Teacher'. That's it. And Jesus has to go off on this tangent about nobody being good but God. I mean, give me a break. Jesus is about as good as they come. But can he take a compliment? Can he just get on with the conversation? Can he make it easy for this guy? No."

"The point, my friend?" the companion interrupted. "What is the point?"

"Yes, well, after all the 'song and dance' about goodness, this fellow asks Jesus what he needs to do to get into the kingdom of heaven. Jesus tells him all the obvious stuff: obey the commandments, love your neighbour, blah, blah, blah. The guy says he's done all that (the rest of us look at each other and roll our eyes – 'Yeah, right!'). But instead of calling him on that, Jesus tells him that there is just one more thing he needs to do. He has to sell everything he has, and give it the poor."

"And…?" the companion asked, leaning even further forward.

"What do you think?" the disciple shrugged. "He walked away."

"And did Jesus go after him?"

"Of course not!" sighed Judas. "He just turned to the rest of us and went on about how hard it is for rich men to get into the kingdom of heaven. 'Harder than squeezing a camel through the eye of a needle.' Those were his exact words."

The companion stroked his chin. "That concerns me," he said seriously. "It doesn't seem right, somehow – theologically, I mean."

Now the disciple leaned forward. "You know, there were a few of us who thought the same thing. I don't know about you, but I have always been taught that wealth is a sign of God's blessing. Not Jesus! He acts like it's some kind of curse."

"Unless one uses it to help the poor," the companion added.

"Well, yes... and no." Judas sighed. "There was this other time. A woman came to Jesus and started to pour this bottle of incredibly expensive perfume on his feet."

"Quite a luxury!" the companion observed.

"Exactly," agreed Judas. "And the first thing that came to my mind was our little treasury. We needed funds desperately, and I, of all people, knew that."

"What with you being the treasurer?" the companion interrupted.

"Just so. Anyway, I knew that I would get nowhere if I suggested selling the perfume and putting the profits in our money-bag. So I simply suggested that we sell it and give the money (well, some of the money!) to the poor. Fool-proof, I thought – a perfectly reasonable plan. But, no! Jesus has a different idea. 'The poor will always be with us,' he says, 'but I am only going to be here for a short while.' (Who knows what he meant by that?!) 'So leave the woman alone and let her get on with it.'

"Now you tell me. Is there any consistency in that, whatsoever? Anything sensible? Anything practical? On the one hand, he accepts this expensive gift. On the other, he condemns rich men for their wealth."

The companion shook his head. "It makes no sense to me – particularly since there are rich men who belong to your little band of followers. What about Levi, the one they call Matthew?"

Judas rolled his eyes. "The tax collector. Yes, well, we seem to specialize in those. Matthew. Zacchaeus. But it's always the same drill: Make friends with Jesus. Give all your money away. Pay back the ones you've cheated. Help the poor. And by the time it's over, there's nothing left for our little treasury. And I should know..."

"What with you being the treasurer," the companion said again.

"Exactly!" sighed the disciple. "And if Jesus ever took the time to look into our money-bag, he'd understand what I have to deal with. It takes more than a penny or two to change the world. And besides, I don't trust him."

"Jesus?" asked the companion.

"No! No! Matthew!" replied Judas. "I think he's still in cahoots with the Romans. It makes sense, doesn't it? He collected taxes for the Romans for all those years. And now I catch him taking notes on what we're up to. Watching, listening, and then scribbling things down! He's spying for them, I'm sure of it."

"I can see why you might be concerned," the companion said. "The Romans are a worry."

"The main worry!" Judas cried. "It's why I joined up with Jesus in the first place. If he is the Messiah – and the miracles alone are enough to keep me convinced – then he will eventually destroy the Romans and our land will be free again. I just wish he'd get on with it. Forget all this nonsense about love and forgiveness, for a while, and start dealing with more practical matters – like raising an army and putting together some kind of battle plan…"

"And finding the money," the companion added.

"And finding the money," Judas sighed.

"This is dangerous talk," the companion whispered. Then he leaned forward and whispered more quietly still, so that his whisper sounded almost like a hiss. "But I think I may have a way to help you."

"Really?" the disciple whispered back.

"Yes," the companion hissed. "Some of my employers in the High Priest's office would like to have a word with Jesus. Privately. They, too, are concerned about the direction his mission has taken and feel that if they could just spend some time alone with him, they might be able to get him back on the right track. If you could lead them to some quiet spot where they could meet with him, I am sure that they would reward you handsomely."

"How handsomely?" Judas asked.

The companion smiled. "I keep forgetting that I am dealing with a practical man here, my friend." And then he paused and then he thought. He had the look of a man bartering for some great treasure. "What would you say to, oh, thirty pieces of silver?"

Judas's eyes lit up. "I would say, 'You have a deal!'" he grinned.

The companion stood and reached out his hand. Judas took it and was surprised by how smooth and slippery it felt.

"So I can count on you?" the companion asked.

"Of course," Judas answered. "At the first opportunity. And the money…?"

"You can trust me for that." The companion smiled. "Cross my heart."

It was an expression that Judas had never heard before. But he didn't think about it long. For as his friend walked away, the disciple had other things to consider. Plans and programmes and practical matters.

"Thirty pieces of silver," he mused. "Now with that kind of money, I can really make a difference in the world!"

Questions

1. So was Jesus not practical? What do you think?

2. There has been a lot of speculation about Judas's motives for betraying Jesus. What do you think?

3. Talk about a time when you or your church had to choose between doing something practical and some other choice. Is "practical" always negative?

Surely Not I, Lord!

(Luke 22:14–23; Matthew 26:17–30)

Introduction

At Spring Harvest 2009, the artists painted a huge version of Da Vinci's *The Last Supper*, during one of the evening meetings. The moment that *The Last Supper* pictures is the moment after Jesus has told his disciples that one of them will betray him, and they all ask, "Is it I?" I thought it was a good time for everyone else to reflect on that question, as well.

> **TELLING TIPS: I think it would be helpful for you to show *The Last Supper* on the screen, explain what's going on in the picture and then do this reading. It would work nicely during a communion service.**

Surely not I, Lord.
It was a mistake, that's all. I never meant for it to become a habit.

Surely not I, Lord.
Everyone else was doing it.

Surely not I, Lord.
I only thought it. I never actually said it.

Surely not I, Lord.
I was only speaking the truth.

Surely not I, Lord.
It was wrong, I know, but she deserved it.

Surely not I, Lord.
They tell me it's no longer a sin.

Surely not I, Lord.
I felt so bad. It made me feel better.

Surely not I, Lord.
I can't be expected to help everyone!

Surely not I, Lord.
At least I did the honest thing.

Surely not I, Lord.
I was really in love with her.

Surely not I, Lord.
I didn't know what I was doing.

Surely not I, Lord.
You would have lost your temper, too.

Surely not I, Lord.
You don't have to live with him.

Surely not I, Lord.
She wouldn't shut up!

Surely not I, Lord.
You can't expect me to be perfect!

Surely not I, Lord.
I did it in private.
I did it to someone else.
I didn't think it had anything to do with you.
I didn't think it was any kind of betrayal
of what I stood for, or of the one who stood in my place.

Surely not I, Lord.
Surely not I, Lord.
Surely not I.

Questions

1. Are there any lines in this reading that you think are inappropriate?

2. If you had to pick one or two that resonated with you, which ones would they be?

3. Do we actually betray Jesus sometimes? How?

Three

(Luke 22:54–62)

Introduction

I keep having to remind myself how young these guys were. OK, nineteen or twenty in the first century was probably "older" than it is today, but still, Peter's youth and relative inexperience make this story a lot more understandable. Excusable? That's what Peter had to wrestle with. And I think I know what his answer would be.

TELLING TIPS: One to do on your own.

One.
One man.
One courtyard.
One newly kindled fire.
One servant girl.
"You look like one of his lot," she says.
And Peter – Peter doesn't hesitate for even one minute.
"I don't know him," he says at once.

Two.
Too long waiting.
Too exposed.
Yet too tired and worried and confused to walk away.
And so, a second voice: "I saw you, too. You were with him."
And a second denial in reply: "You're mistaken, man, it wasn't me."

Three.

Three parts to Palestine. And three distinct accents.

"You're a Galilean," says a third man. "Just like Jesus. I can hear it in your voice."

And three thoughts fight for control in Peter's head.

Run. Admit it. Or...

The third choice. "I don't know what you're talking about."

And then, one, the rooster crows.

And, two, Jesus turns and looks at him.

And, three, Peter leaves the courtyard.

And there's no counting the tears that fall from his face.

Questions

1. Does Peter demonstrate any of the bravado here that came out of his mouth at the Last Supper? How?

2. Do you get the idea that Peter is thinking his answers through, calculating potential consequences? Or is he just acting from his "gut" again?

3. What would you do, in this situation?

The Politician's Tale

(Luke 23:1–25)

Introduction

Sometimes, it's hard to know exactly what a biblical character was like. You piece together the information as best you can, but you're still not sure you've captured the person.

Take Pilate, for example, the Roman governor who presided over the trial and execution of Jesus. Some people have seen him as a basically good man who got caught in a difficult situation. Others have pictured him as weak and indecisive. Personally, I think the clue to his character lies in something he said to Jesus.

"I have come to tell the truth," Jesus explained, during his trial. And all Pilate could say, in return, was, "What is truth?"

You see, there are some people who try hard to live by what they believe is true. And there are others who fail to do that. But the really scary people are the ones who don't believe that there is any truth, any right or wrong, at all. They believe in nothing beyond their own survival, ambitions, or desires. I think that's the kind of person Pilate was. And even though you may find him charming and amusing, his disregard for any truth beyond himself may well make him the baddest baddie of them all.

TELLING TIPS: One to read on your own.

Pilate rubbed his hands together and smiled at his new assistant. "Well, then, are we ready to get to work?"

Marcus smiled politely in return and nodded, "Yes, Governor. And may I say what a pleasure it is to be working for someone who truly seems to enjoy his job."

Pilate winked and gave the young man a knowing look. "Excellent!" he grinned. "Butter up the boss on your very first day. Someone's taught you well, my boy."

"No, I meant it, sir," Marcus responded. "Some of my past employers just seemed to be putting in their time – waiting for that next holiday or the retirement villa by the sea."

"Ah yes," Pilate nodded. "I know the type. I've worked for a few myself. But I can assure you that things are different here. I like what I do! It's difficult, sometimes. And it's always risky. But for my money, it's still the best game in town!"

"Game, sir?" asked Marcus.

"What else would you call it?" said Pilate, dropping down into his chair. "Keep the peace. Keep the revenues rolling in. Keep Caesar happy. Those are the official rules."

"And the object of the game, as well," Marcus added.

Pilate chuckled. "No, my boy. The object of the game is for yours truly to keep his job. And, with any luck, to keep climbing up that empire-sized ladder."

Marcus looked a bit confused, now. "But, sir? What about duty? What about justice? What about right and wrong?"

Pilate's chuckle grew into a laugh. "You do have a lot to learn, don't you?" Then he stood up on his chair and stuck his arms straight out from his sides. "I've always thought it was a bit like walking on an aqueduct."

"An aqueduct, sir?"

Pilate peered down at his assistant. "You mean to tell me that you've never walked on an aqueduct? Why, when I was a boy, growing up in the Roman countryside, there was nothing I enjoyed better. My friends and I would climb up on top of the tallest one we could find. The water would be rushing down the middle, faster than any river. But along the stonework at the edge, there was just enough room to walk."

"But wasn't that dangerous, sir?"

"Of course it was dangerous! That was the point! Fall off one side and you'd smash your head on the ground below. Fall off the other side, and the water would carry you halfway to Syria before they could fish you out. But if you held your arms out just right – leaning a little this way and a little that way and watching carefully for which way the wind was blowing – then you could do it, and not get killed.

"That's what it's like being the Governor of Palestine. A little justice here. A little oppression there. A touch of mercy. A hint of brutality. It's all the same really – just so long as you keep your balance. Just so long as you don't fall off."

"And you enjoy that, sir?"

"More than anything, my boy." Pilate grinned. Then he hopped onto the floor and plopped back into his chair. "Every day is different. Every day, an adventure. So let's see what today brings. Secretary!" he called. "Send in the first appointment."

A short, round, bald-headed man stuck his head into the room.

"I'm terribly sorry, Governor," he apologized, "but I'm afraid you're going to have to come into the courtyard for this one. It's another one of their holy days, and they say they'll be defiled if they come into the building."

"Yes, yes," Pilate sighed. "I know the drill."

But the look on Marcus's face suggested that he did not.

"Defiled, sir?" he asked.

"It's a religious thing," Pilate explained. "The Jews are obsessed with this notion that they are God's special people. Which, of course, makes the rest of us somewhat less-than-special. As a result, they are forbidden to have any close contact with us – to come into our homes, for example – for fear that what we have or don't have, or whatever it is that makes us different, might rub off on them and thus render them unfit to participate in their religious rituals. That's the gist, anyway."

"So what do we do?" Marcus asked.

"We humour them," Pilate answered, sticking out his arms again and tippy-toeing forward. "It's all about balance, remember? Our little walk into the courtyard will make the Jewish leaders happy. And, I don't know about you, but I could use the exercise!" And then Pilate chuckled. "As they say, when in Jerusalem…"

"But what do you think they want, sir?" Marcus asked.

"Publius?" Pilate enquired, turning to his secretary.

And the secretary just rolled his eyes. "It's another messiah, Governor."

Pilate clapped his hands together happily. "Excellent! Did you hear that, Marcus? Another messiah! We should be finished by lunch!"

"A messiah, sir?" Marcus asked. "I'm afraid…"

"Yes, of course. You're new." And then Pilate stopped for a moment. "The messiah is a Jewish legend. The Christ. The Anointed One. The King of the Jews. It's all the same, and it all has to do with their belief that, one

208

day, their God will send a powerful leader to set them free from their enemies."

"Their enemies?" asked Marcus. "And that would be...?"

"Us! Yes, that's right," Pilate grinned. "And I take it as a sign of our efficiency as conquerors and overlords that so many of these messiahs have been popping up recently. I suppose we've dealt with – what? – one a month?"

"At least, sir," moaned Publius. "A nuisance, if you ask me, sir."

"Yes, well, you have to deal with the paperwork, don't you? I, on the other hand, only have to deal with the messiahs. And frankly, I find them quite fun!"

"Fun, sir?" asked Publius and Marcus, together.

"Of course! Messiahs come in two basic shapes, you see. The hairy, under-nourished, wide-eyed, fanatically-religious shape. And the 'don't turn your back on me or I'll stick a knife in your neck' political revolutionary shape.

"Now the first kind is no trouble at all. You listen to them rant and rave for a few minutes, and then send them off to be flogged.

"As for your revolutionary types... well, it's the rules of the game, isn't it? Young Marcus...?"

Marcus thought hard. "Umm... Keep the peace. Keep the revenues rolling in... Keep Caesar happy!"

"Excellent! And because your basic revolutionary messiah is all for starting trouble and disrupting trade and booting poor Caesar out of the country, what do you do? You crucify him. Simple as that!"

"And so," Pilate concluded, grinning that grin and rubbing his hands together again, "let's see what kind of messiah we have today!"

As Pilate entered the courtyard, he glanced at the prisoner. The man stood quiet and still. His hair was matted, his eyes tired. It looked as if someone had beaten him up.

Next, he glanced at the crowd, then turned to his assistant and whispered, "All the big shots are here – the Jewish leaders and their council. I'm guessing that we've got your basic religious-type messiah to deal with."

Finally, he turned to the crowd itself. "So tell me. What is this man charged with?"

The accusations shot forth, more fiercely than Pilate had ever heard them before.

"He stirs up the nation!"

"He tells us not to pay our taxes!"

"He says he is Christ – the King!"

"It seems like he's broken all the rules of the game," observed Marcus.

Pilate just nodded. "So you want me to put him to death? Is that it?" Pilate said to the crowd. "Well, let me talk with him, first. It's Roman law that needs to be satisfied here.

"And it will keep them in their place!" he whispered to Marcus.

Pilate took the prisoner aside and looked him straight in his swollen and bloodshot eyes.

"So you're the King of the Jews, then, are you?"

"That's what they say," shrugged the prisoner.

"Look," Pilate answered, "I don't care what they say. What I need to know is what you say. Are you the King of the Jews or not?"

The prisoner sighed, as if he were tired – not from lack of sleep, but for lack of being understood.

"I have a kingdom, yes. But it's not the kind of kingdom you're thinking of. If it were, my followers would be here, fighting for me."

Now it was Pilate's turn to sigh. "So let me get this straight," he continued. "You say you are a king, then?"

"Yes. Yes! But not a king with armies and lands and servants. I was sent to be a different kind of king. A King of Truth!"

"Truth?" chuckled Pilate. "*Truth?* What is truth?" Then he shook his head and walked back to his aide.

"Well?" asked Marcus.

"Well, he's not political – that's for sure. And he doesn't strike me as your typical religious lunatic, either. He's different, I'll grant you that. But he doesn't deserve to die."

And that's what Pilate told the crowd, "I find no crime, here. No crime at all."

But if Pilate thought that would satisfy them, then he was wrong. They started shouting again – louder even than the first time.

"But he's stirring up the people! It started up in Galilee, and now it's spread all the way down here to Judea."

"They obviously hate this man," Pilate whispered to Marcus. "And they're not going to go away until I do something…" And then Pilate grinned and snapped his fingers.

"Did you say he's from Galilee?" Pilate shouted to the crowd. "Well, that's not under my control. Herod's in charge of Galilee, and as it happens, he's here, in town, for your festival. Why don't you take the prisoner to Herod and let him decide what to do?"

The crowd grunted and moaned. But they were eager to have their way, so they grabbed the prisoner and dragged him off to see Herod.

"There's another lesson for you," Pilate beamed. "When you're having trouble making a decision – or when a decision is likely to make trouble for you – pass the responsibility on to someone else!"

Pilate escorted Marcus back into his office, but it wasn't long before Publius stuck his head into the room again.

"It's that messiah, Governor. I'm afraid he's back."

"But what about Herod?" Pilate asked.

"It seems he's learned that lesson about passing on difficult cases, too," said Marcus.

"Then he's a smarter man than I've given him credit for," Pilate noted. "I'll have to have him over some time." Then he marched out into the courtyard, looking as "official" as possible.

"I have already made my decision," he announced to the crowd. "This man has committed no crime!"

But the crowd would not be pacified, and they shouted even more loudly.

"All right. All right!" Pilate announced. "How about this? Every year, during your festival, I release a prisoner, as a gesture of good will towards the community. What say I let this man go?"

"No!" shouted one of the priests. "Free Barabbas, instead!"

"Barabbas?" asked Marcus.

"A thief and a murderer," explained Pilate, "And also something of a local hero."

And that was why the crowd began to chant, "We want Barabbas! We want Barabbas! We want Barabbas!"

"Ah well," sighed Pilate, "I hate to do it, but it's the rules of the game... All right, then," he announced to the crowd, 'I shall set Barabbas free!" And then he pointed to the prisoner. "But what shall I do with this man?"

"Crucify him!" the crowd chanted. "Crucify him!"

"But he's done nothing wrong!" Pilate called back.

"He's made himself a king!" someone shouted. "And that makes him an enemy of the true king – Caesar!"

"Yes," shouted someone else, "so if you set him free, that makes you Caesar's enemy, too!"

"The hypocrites!" Pilate muttered to Marcus. "They hate Caesar, maybe even more than they hate this man. But it's obvious. They're willing to say anything that will get him crucified. And frankly, I can't afford to let this crowd get any further out of hand. And so I suppose that it comes down to the rules of the game, once again."

"Even if you have to execute an innocent man?" asked Marcus.

Pilate smiled. "Well, I've thought of a way 'round that, as well. Publius, fill me a wash-basin. And bring me a clean towel."

"Do you see this?" called Pilate to the crowd. "I am innocent of this man's blood!" Then he plunged his hands into the water, and ordered his soldiers to beat the prisoner and take him off to be crucified.

"Nice touch, don't you think?" remarked Pilate, once the crowd had gone. "If I've made the right decision, then I'm the hero. And if I've made the wrong one, well, I think I'm covered there, as well."

Marcus was not convinced. "But don't you worry that it makes you seem weak and indecisive?"

"Not if I keep my balance!" smiled Pilate, sticking out his arms again. "Now let's get back to work."

The rest of the day was mainly uneventful.

Some of the Jewish leaders complained about the sign that had been tacked on the prisoner's cross. Someone else came by to claim the man's body once he'd died. And, somewhere in the middle of the afternoon, the weather suddenly turned worse than anyone could remember.

"Well, what do you say, Marcus?" asked Pilate, as they prepared, at last, to go home. "A good day's work?"

"I suppose so, sir," Marcus answered. "But I can't help feeling just a little uncomfortable. I mean, we released a murderer, and executed what looked like an innocent man."

"Yes, that's true," Pilate said. "But did we win the game? That's the important question. And if you look at it that way, we did extraordinarily well. We kept the peace. We prevented a riot..."

"And the dead man, sir?"

"Ah, yes," mused Pilate. "The dead man. Well, I don't think we'll be hearing from him again. Do you?"

Questions

1. What do you think of this portrayal of Pilate? Is it accurate as far as the biblical account goes?

2. How about the "imagined bits"? A fair guess, or would you have done it differently?

3. Why do you suppose so much attention is paid in the Gospels to Pilate's decision and the manner in which it was made?

Travail

(Luke 23:26–46)

Introduction

This is another one of those readings that juxtapose two familiar stories in the hope of making better sense of each of them.

> **TELLING TIPS: You will need two readers: Number 1 – a woman, preferably, for Mary. And Number 2 – a male, for Jesus. This will take some practising to be done well.**

1:	It was a long journey.
2:	It was a hard journey.
1:	Step by agonizing step.
2:	Desperate for a rest.
1:	There were stops, sure.
2:	But not for long.
1:	They just kept going.
2:	On and on.
1:	Until they arrived.
2:	At last!
1:	The place was crowded. No room.
2:	And then, there it was, the spot.
1:	So she lay herself down.
2:	And so did he.
1 & 2:	And, oh, the agony!
1:	The pain came sharp and fast.
2:	One, two, three bursts – in quick succession.
1:	And then, that dropping feeling.
2:	The sudden jolt of it.

1:	The surprise.
2:	The shock.
1:	More waiting followed.
2:	Hour after hour.
1:	And more pain.
2:	So much to bear.
1:	And then, when it seemed like it would never be over,
2:	Never ever end,
1 & 2:	It happened.
1:	And the angels burst forth.
2:	And the angels held back.
1 & 2:	As he opened his mouth and cried.
2:	"Father, into your hands I commit my spirit."
1:	And his eyes opened.
2:	And his eyes shut.
1:	And it began.
2:	And it was done.
1 & 2:	And his mother bowed her head and wept.

Questions

1. What similarities and differences do you see between the sacrifice of Jesus and Mary's sacrifice?

2. Are there any other elements – experiences that the two of them had in common – that you would add to this retelling?

The Thief's Tale

(Luke 23:32–43)

Introduction

Some people say that your whole life flashes before your eyes just before you die. I don't know if that's true or not, because I've never faced that situation! But what if it were true? And what if you had the chance to write it down, or tell it to someone? Then it might sound something like the story you are about to read.

TELLING TIPS: Yet another one to do on your own.

It wasn't my fault. Not really. My brother was older than me. And, you know how it is. You look up to your brother, especially when you're little. And you want to do what he does…

Well, my brother was a thief. And even though he was only eleven or twelve when he started, he got good fast. He had this innocent face, for a start – round chubby cheeks that old ladies just loved to pinch. So they trusted him.

He was quick, too. He could snatch a coin off a table so fast that it looked like his hand had never moved at all!

And, best of all, he could talk. Boy, could he talk! One story after another – lie after lie after lie. And all the time with that smile on his face. My brother could talk his way out of anything!

Once – and I had nothing to do with this, I swear! – once he stole this chicken from old Simeon's wife. And not just any chicken, of course. But her favourite chicken. The one with the big red spot on its back! So, there he was, running down the street, with this chicken tucked under his arm, when who should come bustling out of a door in front of us but the old lady, herself!

Now, Simeon's wife was the chief cheek-pincher in our village. So when she saw my big brother, right there in front of her, she threw wide her huge arms, and like some enormous lobster, began to flex those fat pinching fingers. Escape? Escape was out of the question, for Simeon's wife was also the widest woman in town. We tried to avoid her. We really did. But our speed and her bulk resulted in one huge collision – and my brother and I found ourselves sitting, dazed, on our backsides before her!

"Now where are you boys off to in such a hurry?" she grinned, pinching his cheeks (and then mine, for good measure). But before either of us could say a thing, she spotted her spotty hen.

The big woman's smile turned down into a frown. But before it could fall into a full-fledged scowl, my brother blurted out, "We were bringing your chicken back to you. That's why we were in such a hurry! We found it in… Anna's yard. That's right! And we thought maybe it had wandered there or – God forbid! – that old Anna had stolen your chicken. Anyway, we watched her, and when she went into her house, we grabbed it as fast as we could and ran and – here! – it's all yours again!"

Simeon's wife just looked at my brother, and then, slowly, her frown turned into a puzzled stare.

"But, Anna?" she pondered. "Why would Anna want to take my chicken?"

"Jealousy!" my brother jumped back in, eager to save his story. "That has to be it. After all, it's not everyone who has a chicken that looks like that!"

"That's true," the old woman nodded. And then she leaned near and whispered, "And I'm sure you're too young to know this, but they say that Anna has always fancied my Simeon – the most handsome man in the village, if I say so myself!"

So she bought the story. And instead of smacking us round the head or dragging us off to the local judge, she pinched our cheeks one more time and rewarded us each with a shiny silver coin!

My brother grinned and strutted as we made our way back home. But I was still a little worried.

"What if she talks to Anna?" I said.

"Oh, I don't think that's going to happen," he chuckled, as he pulled a piece of woven cloth out from under his shirt. "I grabbed this out of the old lady's basket," he laughed, "between all the pinching and hugging. It's her own special pattern, and when it gets dark, I know just what we're going to do with it!"

"But it's the Sabbath!" I said.

"That's right!" he grinned again. "Everybody will be at home, praying and reading and stuff. Everybody but you and me!"

And so, later that night, we crept out of our house and across the village and into Anna's yard. And while I watched, my brother quietly wrung the neck of every chicken in her yard, and left that piece of cloth behind as "evidence". (Did I mention that he could be vicious, as well?)

There was a lot of commotion in the village, the next morning – questions and rumours and accusations. And I understand that the two women never talked to one another again.

As for my brother, he just got better and better at his chosen profession. Pick-pocketing, sheep-stealing, breaking and entering – there wasn't anything he couldn't do. And soon, we'd built up a little gang. (Well, he did, actually, because, as I've said, I never did any of the real stealing. I was a lookout, mostly. Just along for the ride.)

We started moving from place to place. We hit the villages first because they were the easiest. But as folk started to recognize us, we had to aim for the larger towns, and then the cities. Get lost in the crowds – you know what I mean.

Crowds can be a great cover, actually. That's what my brother always said. All those people, bunched together – jostling, bumping, pushing. And if a hand should slip into a pocket, a pouch, or a purse, who would notice? Markets are good, public executions aren't bad, but nothing beats a good old-fashioned religious festival! Nobody's on their guard, you see. They're all feeling good and holy, and they walk around with the mistaken notion that everyone else is feeling good and holy, too!

There was this time, for example, up in Galilee – near the sea, I think – when all these people were listening to this teacher. His name was Jesus and he was another one of those Messiah wannabes. You know – "Follow me and I will lead you to God." That sort of thing. Anyway, we were doing pretty well. The crowd couldn't keep its eyes off him, which meant, of course, that they weren't paying attention to us at all!

He was telling this story, about a guy who gets fed up with his dad, runs off with his inheritance, and gambles it all away – or something like that. When the money's all gone, this guy drags himself back home again. You know what the father's going to do – smack him round the head (like

Simeon's wife should have done to us!). But, no! The father rewards him – gives him rings and robes and a fancy feast! I have to admit, it was the most unlikely story I had ever heard. So I glanced over at my brother, to get his reaction. And he was fuming!

I thought, for a moment that he was angry with me – for listening to the story instead of, you know, attending to the "business". But it was the teacher – that's who had him so worked up.

"Now there's the thief!" he muttered. "He doesn't work – I can promise you that. But somebody's feeding him and taking care of him. He fills their heads with lies, and they love him for it. Let's get out of here!"

And so, even though there were hundreds of purses left to pinch, we headed out across the hills and into the nearest town.

A couple of years went by – I was about eighteen or nineteen by then – and we started to get a little cocky. Success does that to you, and the problem is that you start to get sloppy, too. Soon you start to believe that you can pull off anything – even stealing from the Romans.

That was our big mistake. If we'd stuck to Jews and Samaritans and the odd caravan trader, we'd still be working today. But someone told my brother about all the jewellery hidden away in this centurion's house, down in Jerusalem. So he planned it, he broke in, and he grabbed it. (And as for his beating the centurion nearly to death, well, I can't say, can I? I was outside. The lookout. Remember?) Anyway, what we didn't know was that the old boy was retiring, and that a bunch of soldiers had chosen that very night to surprise him with a party. So the surprise was on us and, surrounded, we surrendered. What else could we do?

My brother tried to talk his way out of it. But the Romans didn't really understand our language. So instead of a pinch on the cheek, all he got was a punch in the mouth. Then they dragged us off to jail.

When he came to, my brother just sat there, speechless, not for hours, but for days. I'd never seen him so quiet, but each time I tried to say something – you know, start up a conversation, lighten the mood – he growled at me. And, I got the message.

Finally, he spoke. But it wasn't what I expected him to say.

"Did you ever wish you could start all over again?"

I was a little confused. "You mean, like planning the robbery better? Or staying away from the Romans?"

"No," he sighed. "I mean – life. Starting over again. Getting another chance. Like the story that teacher told, about the boy and his father. You remember?"

"But you thought that was stupid," I reminded him.

"Yeah, well, I guess I never thought I'd need a second chance. I was always so good at talking my way out of things. But now, now that it's all over, I guess I feel different."

"What do you mean, 'all over'?" I asked. "We're getting out of here, right?"

And that's when he gave me "the look". The big brother to little brother "look". The look that said he thought I was some kind of an idiot.

"You don't get it, do you?" he said. "They're going to kill us. These are the Romans we're talking about. They're going to drag us out of here, hang us on a cross, and crucify us!"

"But why?" I asked. "Why? I mean, I didn't do anything. I was just the lookout. You can tell them that, can't you?"

But my brother just sighed and shook his head and turned his face again, silent, to the wall.

He was right, of course. Not two days later, they woke us up, tied each of us to a cross, and before the sun came up, there we were, just hanging there, waiting to die.

I screamed for a little while. "It's not my fault," I pleaded. "It's not fair!"

But the soldiers just laughed, and the growing crowd didn't want to know. So after a while, I shut up. It was hard to breathe, hanging like that, and harder still to talk. Maybe that's why my brother never said a word.

Time passed. I don't know how much. And then a whole parade of people came marching up the hill. There was wailing and weeping on one side and cheering on the other. And then they propped a third cross up between us.

I turned my head and looked at the guy. He was a mess! Cuts and bruises all over his body, and blood pouring down his face. He must have done something awful, I thought. And as bad as I felt, I was glad I wasn't in his shoes.

And then I looked closer, at the sign tacked above his head. And I couldn't believe what I saw.

It was Jesus! You know, the teacher we saw up in Galilee!

I tried to get my brother's attention. But, no, he wouldn't even look my way. So I thought, hey, why not try to win a little respect from him, cheer him up, maybe, right at the end? Show him that I'm not the idiot brother he always thought I was.

So I turned to this Jesus and I said, "Hey. Hey! They say you're the Messiah, right? God's Special Guy. Well, if you're such a big shot, why don't you do something about this? Why don't you snap your fingers or say the magic word and get us all out of this mess?"

It was good, I thought. Funny, you know. So I glanced at my brother, just to get his reaction. And I couldn't believe it – he was giving me that "idiot" look again!

"What is wrong with you?" he sighed. "We're all going to die here. Aren't you afraid of that? And aren't you even more afraid of God, and what he'll do to us? I mean, we're here because we deserve it. We've been thieves all our lives. But look at this man. Look at him! He's done nothing wrong. Not a thing."

And then he turned to the teacher. And I don't know – maybe it was just sweat – but I'd swear there were tears in my brother's eyes. And that's when he said it.

"Jesus. Jesus, will you remember me when you come into your kingdom?"

And Jesus nodded. And Jesus forced a little smile. And Jesus said, "Yes. Today, truly, you will be with me in paradise."

Yeah, I know what you're thinking. I suppose I should have said something, too. But, hey, what for? It was my brother, my brother who was the bad guy. My brother who was the thief. I was just a lookout. Honest. I never did anything wrong, not really. Like I said at the beginning, It wasn't my fault…

Questions

1. OK, so this one is almost entirely made up. Does it work? Why or why not?

2. Do you know anyone who never takes the blame for anything – who always thinks their troubles are someone else's fault? What's it like to have to deal with that kind of person?

3. Is there hope for someone who honestly believes they haven't done all that much wrong, and therefore sees no need for forgiveness?

A Resurrection Rhyme

(Luke 24)

Introduction

Couldn't finish without one last rhyming story!

TELLING TIPS: See "Mary Meets an Angel" (above) for suggestions on how to tell this kind of story.

The women were walking in the early morning light.
The women were walking in the early morning light.
The women were walking in the early morning light.
They were off to visit a tomb.
(Make shape of tomb with fingers – round or gravestone-shaped.)
They were off to visit a tomb.
They were off to visit a tomb.

Their friend Jesus was dead and they were very sad.
Their friend Jesus was dead and they were very sad.
Their friend Jesus was dead and they were very sad.
Their hearts were filled with gloom.
(Make sad face.)
Their hearts were filled with gloom.
Their hearts were filled with gloom.

Then the ground beneath them began to shake,
Then the ground beneath them began to shake,
Then the ground beneath them began to shake,
And then there was an earthquake – kaboom!
(Shake body, like in an earthquake.)

And then there was an earthquake – kaboom!
And then there was an earthquake – kaboom!

And when they looked and they saw – the grave was open.
And when they looked and they saw – the grave was open.
And when they looked and they saw – the grave was open.
They were staring in the face of doom.
(Open-mouthed, horrified expression.)
They were staring in the face of doom.
They were staring in the face of doom.

Then two angels appeared – right out of nowhere,
Then two angels appeared – right out of nowhere,
Then two angels appeared – right out of nowhere,
And said, "You're looking for your friend, We assume."
(Finger to chin, as if thinking.)
And said, "You're looking for your friend, We assume."
And said, "You're looking for your friend, We assume."

"Your friend Jesus is alive!" the angels told the women.
"Your friend Jesus is alive!" the angels told the women.
"Your friend Jesus is alive!" the angels told the women.
"He's walked out of this dead man's room."
(Make square shape of room with fingers.)
"He's walked out of this dead man's room."
"He's walked out of this dead man's room."

And that's when Jesus appeared and the women cried for joy,
And that's when Jesus appeared and the women cried for joy,
And that's when Jesus appeared and the women cried for joy,
Like a bride looking at her groom.
(Clasp hands, tilt head, stare lovingly at person sitting next to you.)
Like a bride looking at her groom.
Like a bride looking at her groom.

"Go tell all my friends," said Jesus to the women,
"Go tell all my friends," said Jesus to the women,
"Go tell all my friends," said Jesus to the women,

"That I'm alive and I'll be seeing them soon."
(Look at wrist as if there is a watch there and tap it.)
"That I'm alive and I'll be seeing them soon."
"That I'm alive and I'll be seeing them soon."

So the women ran off to tell all their friends
So the women ran off to tell all their friends
So the women ran off to tell all their friends
Far away from that empty tomb.
(Repeat first motion)
Far away from that empty tomb.
Far away from that empty tomb.

Questions

1. Put yourself in the place of the women. What is going through your mind as you walk to the tomb?

2. What about when you see the angels?

3. And then Jesus himself?

Women!

(Luke 24:1–12)

Introduction

It's the little phrases, that usually just slide by in the text, the ones that get you thinking when you finally take the time to consider just what they mean – it's one of those phrases that kicked off this reading.

> **TELLING TIPS: Do it on your own – with feeling. Or you might like to make it a radio play kind of thing – to bring out the different characters.**

"What do you mean, you don't believe us?" sobbed Mary Magdalene. "We were there!"

"You're upset," said John. "Look at you. It's been a very difficult few days. No one could blame you for getting a little... hysterical."

"We're not hysterical!" shrieked Joanna.

"We can see that," said James, winking at the others.

Joanna lowered her register, more than a few notches, and then, slowly and deliberately, she said, "We are not hysterical because of what we saw. We are hysterical because you won't believe us!"

"We don't believe you," said Peter, even more slowly, "because dead people don't come back from the grave."

"Lazarus did!" countered the other Mary. "And that boy from Nain. And Jairus's daughter!"

"Because Jesus was there to bring them back from the dead," replied Peter, more slowly still, like he was talking to an imbecile.

"That's right," added Andrew, desperate to help. "Jesus brought them back from the dead when he was alive. So now that he's dead, he can't bring anybody back to life, particularly himself, because he's dead. And not alive... to... to... bring himself back... to life... from... the dead. I think."

"You don't have to spell it out for us," sighed Mary Magdalene. "We're not stupid. But we saw what we saw. Why don't you just believe us?"

"It was dark when you arrived, wasn't it?" asked Peter.

And the women nodded.

"And you were upset. So surely there was a part of you that *wanted* to see him alive again."

"And that's why you imagined it," Nathaniel concluded. "Nothing wrong with that."

"Imagined an open tomb?" asked Joanna incredulously.

"And a blinding light? And angels?" said Mary Magdalene.

"And what about the rest?" added the other Mary. "What they said – all those things about Jesus being delivered into the hands of sinful men and being crucified and returning on the third day. It sounds like a lot of what Jesus himself said!"

"Jesus said a lot of... symbolic... things," countered Peter. "And the fact that you remembered one or two of them still doesn't prove that he's alive."

"We saw it! Every one of us!" cried Mary Magdalene. "What other proof do you need? Why won't you just believe us?"

Peter sighed. "All right, then. How about this. How about I go to the tomb and have a little look round?"

"I don't know," said John. "There are soldiers everywhere out there. I don't think it's safe."

"Oh, terrific – but it was all right for us to go?" said Joanna, in a huff.

"Well, you're just, you know – women," said Andrew, trying hard again. "It's different with us men. The soldiers wouldn't be looking... for ..." And then he looked around. The women's arms were crossed in front of them. The men were looking at the ceiling. Someone was whistling. "And... and... maybe this isn't the time," he finished.

"I'm going," said Peter. "If the soldiers get me..."

"No, no... they won't," added the other Mary. "There was an earthquake as well – I remember it now – it knocked them out."

"Very convenient," Peter sighed. "It gets better with every telling. So as I said, I'm off. Pray I get back in one piece."

So Peter left. And Peter went to the tomb. And what he found were strips of linen, lying on their own. So he went away, wondering. But sometime later that day, says Luke, Jesus appeared to him, alive!

What did Jesus say? We don't know. But there's a part of me that would like to think that the first thing he did was to put his hand on his friend's shoulder, lean over, and whisper in his ear:

"The women, Peter. Why didn't you just believe what they said?"

Questions

1. Why didn't the disciples believe the women? What do you think?

2. Would you have believed them? Why or why not?

3. Of course, there are loads of people who still don't believe them! What would your response be to those people?

Emmaus

(Luke 24:11–35)

Introduction

One last rhyming story!

> **TELLING TIPS: See "Mary Meets and Angel" (above) for suggestions on how to tell this kind of story.**

Cleopas and his mate were walking to Emmaus.
Cleopas and his mate were walking to Emmaus.
Cleopas and his mate were walking to Emmaus.
They were sad because their friend Jesus was dead.
(Make some sort of "dead" motion – hands round throat, or whatever.)
They were sad because their friend Jesus was dead.
They were sad because their friend Jesus was dead.

Then suddenly Jesus joined them, right there on the road,
Then suddenly Jesus joined them, right there on the road,
Then suddenly Jesus joined them, right there on the road,
But they thought that he was someone else instead.
(Hold out one hand then the other.)
But they thought that he was someone else instead.
But they thought that he was someone else instead.

"What's going on?" asked Jesus, as he matched his pace to theirs.
"What's going on?" asked Jesus, as he matched his pace to theirs.
"What's going on?" asked Jesus, as he matched his pace to theirs.
And Cleopas and his mate just shook their heads.
(Shake head.)

And Cleopas and his mate just shook their heads.
And Cleopas and his mate just shook their heads.

"Jesus died," Cleopas sighed. "He was our Saviour, so we thought.
"Jesus died," Cleopas sighed. "He was our Saviour, so we thought.
"Jesus died," Cleopas sighed. "He was our Saviour, so we thought.
It's over now, his followers have fled."
(Turn quickly, like you're about to dash away or look for a place to hide.)
It's over now, his followers have fled."
It's over now, his followers have fled."

"Wait," added his mate, "some people say that he's alive.
"Wait," added his mate, "some people say that he's alive.
"Wait," added his mate, "some people say that he's alive.
But you know what it's like when rumours spread."
(Wave hands in a spreading motion.)
But you know what it's like when rumours spread."
But you know what it's like when rumours spread."

"Dead? Alive again? That's how it's s'posed to be," said Jesus.
"Dead? Alive again? That's how it's s'posed to be," said Jesus.
"Dead? Alive again? That's how it's s'posed to be," said Jesus.
"It's in the prophets, which it seems you've never read."
(Pretend to read book or scroll.)
"It's in the prophets, which it seems you've never read."
"It's in the prophets, which it seems you've never read."

So he taught them from the law and he taught them from the prophets,
So he taught them from the law and he taught them from the prophets,
So he taught them from the law and he taught them from the prophets,
Until Emmaus town lay dead ahead.
(Point straight ahead.)
Until Emmaus town lay dead ahead.
Until Emmaus town lay dead ahead.

"It's getting late," the two friends said. "Please stay with us tonight.
"It's getting late," the two friends said. "Please stay with us tonight.
"It's getting late," the two friends said. "Please stay with us tonight.

You'll need something to eat. You'll need a bed."
(Head on hands, like sleeping.)
You'll need something to eat. You'll need a bed."
You'll need something to eat. You'll need a bed."

They all sat down for supper, a simple meal but good.
They all sat down for supper, a simple meal but good.
They all sat down for supper, a simple meal but good.
Jesus bowed his head, gave thanks, and broke the bread.
(Pretend to break bread.)
Jesus bowed his head, gave thanks, and broke the bread.
Jesus bowed his head, gave thanks, and broke the bread.

"It's him!" the two friends cried – and just like that he'd gone
"It's him!" the two friends cried – and just like that he'd gone
"It's him!" the two friends cried – and just like that he'd gone
With nothing left behind – not a shred.
(Hold up tiny pretend bit of something.)
With nothing left behind – not a shred.
With nothing left behind – not a shred.

So they went back to Jerusalem, more quickly than they'd come.
So they went back to Jerusalem, more quickly than they'd come.
So they went back to Jerusalem, more quickly than they'd come.
They raced, they ran, they skipped, they flew, they sped.
(Pretend to run.)
They raced, they ran, they skipped, they flew, they sped.
They raced, they ran, they skipped, they flew, they sped.
To tell their friends that Jesus was not dead!

Questions

1. Why do you think they did not recognize Jesus?

2. What bits of the law and the prophets do you know that suggest the Messiah will die and live again?

3. What significance is there (if any) to the fact that they recognized Jesus when he broke the bread? Were they at the Last Supper? Or is there more to this?

The Fisherman's Tale

(John 21)

Introduction

Sometimes the worst kind of badness is the badness inside you, the badness you can't seem to fix. You say something hurtful to somebody. Or you lose your temper. Or you lie about something. And a minute after you do it, you feel bad, and you wish you could take it all back. But you can't, because you're embarrassed or afraid or worried that something worse might happen if you try to put it right.

Everybody feels that way, sometimes. Peter did. He was one of Jesus' followers, one of his closest friends. But time and time again, he found himself doing and saying things that disappointed Jesus – things he was sorry for, later. This story is about one of those times. And even though Peter tried, he still couldn't find a way to fix and forgive himself. He needed someone to do it for him. And fortunately, that someone was there, hanging on a cross, rising from the dead, and waiting for him, on the beach.

TELLING TIPS: One more to read on your own.

The fire was warm. And the end of his beard and the edge of his sandals were just about dry.

His belly was full. The taste of fish lingered in his mouth, and his moustache clung to a crusty bit of bread.

He'd just had a big catch. His friends sat round about him. He should have been happy. But he wasn't.

His best friend of all was there, you see. The one who had died and come back to life. The one he had abandoned and denied.

There had been a fire, then, as well. And a cold night. And a silent moon. And in the place of the comrades who now chattered around him, there sat strangers and enemies.

Peter remembered it well. Too well. It was a serving girl who spoke first. She had been gazing through the flames for some time, trying to catch his eye and a good look at his face. But Peter had sat still, still as stone – hunched over, silent, afraid. It was her voice that set him shivering.

"This man was with him, too!" she pointed. "With Jesus, who they arrested!"

Peter held himself tight, to stop the shaking. He was afraid. He was afraid! The guards. The arrest. The torches. The fighting. His friends were scattered, his master in custody. He was afraid! Who wouldn't be? And surely that was why he had blurted it out, almost without thinking – "Woman! I do not know the man!"

It was a lie. Of course it was a lie! But if that busybody hadn't stuck her nose in…

Before he could fashion his excuse, however, another voice called out from the darkness.

"Yes, you're right. I've seen him with Jesus, too! You're one of his followers, aren't you?"

"No. No!" Peter shouted, wishing that somehow he could disappear, hoping to heaven that he could just wake up from this nightmare. "No, I am not one of them!"

But the strangers would not be quiet. They would not give up. He was the focus of attention, now. And all eyes – he could feel them – were gazing, peering, inspecting and identifying, each and every one trained on him.

Jesus' career had been so public, the miracles so amazing, the crowds so huge. Thousands and thousands of people had seen them together, with Peter the biggest and noisiest of the bunch. And so it was inevitable that another voice, a third voice, should come to the same conclusion as the rest.

"Yes!" someone called. "Definitely! He's from Galilee. He's one of them!"

"No!" shouted Peter, his heart racing and his hands sweating.

"No!" he repeated, frantic and afraid.

"I never even knew the man!"

And then the rooster crowed.

Jesus had said this would happen. In the midst of Peter's boasting about how he would fight to the death for his master, Jesus had contradicted him.

"No, Peter," he had whispered, "before this night is through, before the cock calls to the coming dawn, you will deny that you ever knew me."

Peter wept bitterly, that day, mixing his tears with the morning dew. And he could find no excuse – not fear, not panic, not fate – to chase away the guilt he felt at turning his back on his friend.

A chunk of wet sand, caked to the side of his leg, dried through just enough to fall off. But it left behind a filmy, sandy residue that irritated him until he brushed it away. And Peter couldn't help thinking that it was just the same way with his guilt.

They'd met a few times – he and Jesus – since that night before Jesus had died. But now, Jesus was alive again! And the shock and the joy of those meetings had shaken away great chunks of Peter's guilt and shame. But it wasn't all gone. And Jesus hadn't mentioned it. And Peter didn't want to bring it up.

And that's why this man with a full belly and warm feet and one amazing, resurrected friend wasn't very happy. There was something he needed to do. Something he couldn't bring himself to say.

There was another reason, too: fish.

When they'd first met – he and Jesus – Peter was a fisherman. But Jesus had promised to make him something else – a fisher of men. More than that, Jesus had called him a rock, and when Peter had found the confidence to stand up and say what all the disciples had been thinking – that Jesus was the Messiah – he had received the master's praise for his insight.

But where was Peter, now? Sitting on the sand at the side of Lake Galilee. That's where he was. Back where he had started, doing his old job, fishing for fish. But what else was he fit for? What good was a rock that turned to sand at the first whiff of danger?

And how could he be a fisher of men when he'd been afraid to admit his allegiance to Jesus to even three people? Perhaps a fisher of fish was all he was good for, after all.

A gull cried. The fire popped. Then it belched out a puff of smoke. Jesus watched the smoke melt into the air, then he turned to Peter and said, "Simon, son of John, do you love me more than these?"

Surprised by both the suddenness of the question and by the question itself, Peter had to stop and think.

Do I love him more than these? These what? These other disciples? Well, of course I do. Didn't I say once that even if all the others left him, I would remain?

And then Peter hung his head in shame. *But I didn't, did I?* he remembered again. *I ran and hid like everybody else. And worse.*

Meanwhile, Jesus was poking holes in the sand, waiting for an answer. Peter knew what he wanted to say. But after what he'd done, would Jesus believe him, or just think him the worst kind of hypocrite? And so, with his eyes fixed on the sand, he said, both as quietly and as firmly as he could, "Yes, Lord, you know that I love you."

Jesus set the stick down and looked at Peter's face. "Then feed my lambs," he said.

This wasn't the response that Peter expected. He thought that Jesus was finally getting round to the "denial" business. That he'd tell him off, call him a no-good liar or a coward or a phony. Peter could understand that. It was the least he deserved.

Or maybe, on the other hand, Peter imagined, Jesus would turn to him and say, "It's all right. I understand. Don't worry about it any more."

But he didn't do either of those things. All he said was, "Feed my lambs."

And then it dawned on him. Perhaps, when Jesus had said, "Do you love me more than these?" he hadn't meant "these disciples" at all. Perhaps he'd meant "these fish". Well, not the fish themselves, but the fishing gear – the nets and tackle and rope. Maybe Jesus was saying, "Do you really intend to go back to being a fisher of fish? Or do you want to carry on working for me?"

Peter was going to ask, but Jesus got there first. "Simon, son of John," he repeated, "do you love me?"

There was that question again! Perhaps Jesus hadn't heard him the first time. The answer had been rather quiet. But Peter was feeling more confident, now. So he looked at Jesus this time. Well, glanced at him, really. And he gave him the same answer. "Yes, Lord, you know that I love you."

"Then feed my sheep," repeated Jesus in return.

That's it! thought Peter. *He does want me back! He still wants me to be a fisher of men. And he still believes I can be a rock. And now he wants me to be a shepherd, as well – to take care of his followers! He wants me back. He thinks I can do it. Everything is all right again!*

Peter was just about to leap to his feet and throw his nets on the fire, when Jesus leaned forward and asked him, one more time:

"Do you love me?"

Well, this is silly! thought Peter. *We've dealt with that already.* Surely, Jesus had heard him the first two times. What was the point of saying it… a third time?

Peter leaned back, shut his eyes, and sighed. Some rock he was turning out to be. More like rocks-for-brains! Peter saw it all, now. Jesus was giving him his job back, yes. But he was giving him something more: a chance to make up for those other three times. A chance to say what he should have said that night. A chance to speak the truth from his heart. A chance to deal with it, once and for all.

Peter opened his eyes and wiped them dry with the back of his hand. Then he looked right at Jesus, right into his eyes, and said, "Lord, you know everything. You know that I love you."

And in return, Jesus smiled a knowing, everything-will-be-all-right kind of smile, and said, for the third time, "Then feed my sheep."

The fire was warm. His belly was full. He was surrounded by his friends. And now, for the first time in a long time, Peter was happy. Not only because his best friend was alive again. But also because something had come back to life in him, as well.

Questions

1. Bible scholars have often assumed that the three chances Jesus gives Peter to say he loves him are a way of helping Peter to deal with his denial. Are there any other possible explanations?

2. Why does Jesus tell Peter to feed his sheep?

3. Talk about a time when you wished you could somehow "make up" for some awful thing you did or said. What was that like? And is Peter actually "making up" for the denial here? Or is there something else going on?

A Sort of Great Commission Song

(Matthew 28:18–20)

Introduction

This song has the same tune as the "Lovin' God Party" song earlier in the book. It was originally part of a sketch at Spring Harvest that featured Pip, Tommo and Big Bart from my *Best Mates* books. It's silly but fun, and it does get the point across (sort of). The best bit when we originally taught the actions had to do with the variety of baptismal practices represented at the conference. We suggested that, when they sang the line "stick 'em in the water", people should do whatever was appropriate to their tradition. So Baptists should pretend to dunk, Anglicans to sprinkle, etc. We weren't sure what the folks from the Salvation Army should do until one of the members of the Lacey Theatre Company came up with a brilliant idea – harmonize!

> **TELLING TIPS: I think it's pretty self-explanatory. Do the baptism action in the first line. Cross yourself for Spirit, Son and Father in the second line. And in the fourth line, point to self, then to another.**
>
> - **North line – make snowy motions with hand or pretend to slip**
> - **West line – swing pretend lariat above head and yell "Yee-hah!"**
> - **South line – shield face from sun**
> - **East line – pretend to eat sushi with chopsticks**

Make disciples and stick 'em in the water,
In the name of the Spirit, Son and the Father.
Make disciples and stick 'em in the water,
And teach them everything that I taught you.

Tell them in the North – where it's really snowy.
Tell them in the West – where they go "Yee-hah!"
Tell them in the South – where the sun is glow-y.
Tell them in the East – at the sushi bar!

Make disciples and stick 'em in the water,
In the name of the Spirit, Son and the Father.
Make disciples and stick 'em in the water,
And teach them everything that I taught you.

Questions

1. Why do you think Jesus said "disciples" and not "converts"?

2. Have we done a reasonable job of making disciples? What do you think is the key to doing that?

3. And why do you think Jesus put such an emphasis on baptism?